WADSWORTH PHIL(

CW00544469

ON

CONFUCIUS

Peimin Ni
Grand Valley State University

Australia • Canada • Mexico • Singapore • Spain
United Kingdom • United States

WADSWORTH

THOMSON LEARNING™

Printed in the United States of America
  2 3 4 5 6 7 04 03

For permission to use material from this text, contact us:
Web: http://www.thomsonrights.com
Fax: 1-800-730-2215
Phone: 1-800-730-2214

For more information, contact:
Wadsworth/Thomson Learning, Inc.
10 Davis Drive
Belmont, CA 94002-3098
USA
http://www.wadsworth.com

ISBN: 0-534-58385-7

CONTENTS

Preface   1

1. Introduction   3
    Historical Background   4
    The Life of Confucius   5
    A Brief History of Confucianism   7

2. The Unity between Heaven and Human Being   10
    This World vs. Other Worlds   11
    Immanence vs. Transcendence   12
    Anxiety vs. Curiosity   14
    Heart-mind vs. the Intellect   16
    Decision vs. Discovery   18
    Decree of Heaven vs. Fate   20
    Contextual Person vs. Atomistic Individual   23

3. *Ren*—Human Heartedness   27
    The Nature of *Ren*   27
    The "Golden Rule"   29
    "*Shu*"—A Method to Be *Ren*   31
    Love the People   33
    Respectfulness, Reverence, and Leniency   38
    Beneficence   40
    Action and Words   44

4. *Li*—Ritual Propriety   51
    Li as Embodiment of *Ren* and *Yi*   52
    Li as Fabrics of Social Order   57
    Li as Effective Ways of Action   60
    Li as A Vital Constituent of Education   63
    Aesthetic Dimension of *Li*   64

5. *Zheng* —Social and Political Philosophy   **66**
    Harmony vs. Conformity   67
    Internal Sageliness and External Kingliness   68
    Freedom   70
    Democracy   76
    Women's Status   79

6. *Xue*—Learning to be Human   **81**
    Xue—Learning   81
    Si—Thinking   86
    Zhi—Knowing   88
    Zhong Yong—The Mean   91
    Yue—Aesthetic Enjoyment   94

Bibliography   **97**

Acknowledgments

I would like to thank Dr. Daniel Kolak for giving me the motivation to write this book and the encouragement to complete it in a short period of time. Much of the book is based on my lectures on Confucianism in the previous ten years of my teaching career, especially at Grand Valley State University. My colleagues and students have always been an important source of my intellectual stimulation. Particularly I would like to express my gratitude to my colleague Stephen Rowe and my long time friend Geling Shang, for bringing numerous subtle and important points up during our casual conversations about Confucianism and about philosophy and life in general.

I want to express my appreciation to Ms. Cheryl Jones and Professor Dewey Hoitenga for eliminating many errors in the manuscript. The remaining errors, of course, are my own sole responsibility.

My gratitude extends also to my wife Ying Xu and my daughter Sophie, for their understanding and support.

Preface

A few decades ago, one might have thought it difficult to argue for the inclusion of a volume on Confucius in a Philosophers Series, since Confucius was typically portrayed as a spiritual leader or an educator, but not as a philosopher. "Philosophy" is a word that originated from Greek, and Confucius had never heard of it. Many philosophers consider philosophy a rational enterprise requiring, among other things, clear definition of concepts and logical argumentation. Confucius' teachings are mostly fragmental assertions, life stories, and descriptions of his character arranged in apparently no logical order. No wonder books of Confucianism are placed, together with other Eastern literatures, either in the section of "Asian studies," or "religion," or "wisdom books."

Today, the tendency is to consider Confucianism a philosophy. While some would still reject Confucius as a philosopher, many have recognized the considerable similarity between his concerns and those of Western philosophers. But some have gone so far as to portray him as merely a speculative philosopher. They have used Western philosophical concepts to interpret him, classify him, and evaluate him. Consequently, not only have some of his concepts been misinterpreted, but vital dimensions of Confucianism, such as its pedagogical, therapeutic, and religious dimensions have been ignored or rejected as non-essential.

It is therefore a pre-requisite for readers of Confucius' philosophy to have a broader notion of philosophy. If we define the word

1

"philosophy" according to its central concerns, such as the nature of human existence, value, social order, etc., then the method that is used predominantly by Western philosophers should not be considered the only valid method for philosophy. By the same token, nor should the specific questions that Western philosophers address be considered the only questions for philosophy. The value of Confucius' teachings is located no less in his differences from his Western counterparts than in the similarities.

Yet since this book is primarily aimed at contemporary readers who are more or less influenced by Western rationalistic way of thinking, it is necessary for the author to present Confucius in a way that is as familiar to the contemporary Western mind as the subject allows. For that reason, I may speak more than Confucius did to articulate his teachings and reveal his hidden or implied meanings and arguments. The danger is that this may create an impression that one can have an adequate understanding of Confucianism merely by reading this book. But practicing and experiencing what he talks about is as vital to understanding Confucius as seeing a color is to understanding the notion of the color.

I may also create a misleading impression by arranging the presentation systematically under different subject headings, as if there is a linear logical order here. Confucius' teachings are actually interrelated with each other in such a way that they are like different sides of a crystal—each and every side reflects the whole system. That is probably why the whole book of the *Analects*, the "Bible" of Confucianism, consists of excerpts put together with no apparent logical order. It does not matter whether you read it front to back or back to front. One saying of the Master may apply as much to his "metaphysics" as to his view on ethics or his political philosophy. Deep understanding of Confucianism is in part dependent on seeing these interconnections.

In this book I intend to introduce the philosophy that Confucius himself had held. References to other Confucian philosophers are therefore limited to what will enrich and deepen our understanding of Confucius. The translation of the Chinese texts is mostly based on the books listed in the bibliography at the end of this book. In some cases I took the liberty to alter some of the translations, by either retranslating some of the terms, or by combining parts of different translations. The reason for doing this is both for accuracy and for easy comprehension. Citations from Confucius' *Analects* will be given simply in parentheses with the chapter number and the section number. For example, "(2/1)" means chapter 2, section 1 from the book of the *Analects*.

2

1

Introduction

In Qufu, a town that belongs now to Shandong Province in China, there is a huge temple dedicated to Confucius. Among hundreds of stone tablets for honoring Confucius, many were elected by emperors of different dynasties when they came to pay homage to the "King without a Crown." For the past two thousand years, Confucius has been regarded as the founder of one of the world's greatest systems of thought, the supreme sage, and China's greatest teacher. Confucianism has been taken in China as the principles of morality, of law, of government, of education, and of life in general, which everyone is supposed to follow, from the emperor down to the ordinary people. It was what children studied in school, primarily, and what government officials had to master in order to pass imperial qualification examinations. Those who were not able to receive formal education were no less influenced by it. Their life style, their values, and their personal relationships were all supposed to fit within the parameters set by the orthodoxy.

Today, the situation has changed a lot, especially due to the powerful influences from the West. But not only the history is of great interest to historians, nor merely that Confucian influence is still a living reality that the residents of the "global village" can not afford to ignore; the insights contained in Confucius' teachings are of significant value for us to appreciate, as many leading scholars have pointed out. Harvard University Professor Tu Wei-ming, a leading advocator of Confucianism in the world today, says that the world is approaching another upsurge of

3

Confucianism, in which it will be re-appropriated through its encounter and integration with Western intellectual traditions.

Historical Background

The time Confucius lived (551-479 B.C.E.) was known as the Spring and Autumn period, when the glory of the Western Zhou 周 Dynasty was declining, but still in fresh memory in the minds of the people. By that time, China already had thousands of years of civilization. Legends about the remote antiquity when the sage-kings Yao 堯 and Shun 舜 ruled (around 24th to 23rd century B.C.E.) were considered a golden age, a time of great harmony. The subsequent Xia 夏 (21st to 16th century B.C.E.) and Shang 商 (16th -11th century B.C.E.) dynasties both enjoyed long periods of prosperity, but both ended with ruthless tyrants ruling the kingdom.

The Zhou Dynasty (11th -3rd century B.C.E.) began with both deep layers of legacy and profound transitions in both social and political structure and in its ideology. King Wen and his brother Duke Zhou, founders of the Zhou, laid the foundation of a humanitarian government, in emulation of the ancient sage-kings, and refined the feudal ritual system. The kingdom was divided into a large number of feudal states, each governed by close relatives (usually sons or brothers) of the King, the "Son of Heaven" 天子, the bearer of the Decree of Heaven.

Lasted for over five hundred years, Zhou was the longest dynasty in the Chinese history. By the Spring and Autumn period, however, the social order of the Zhou was crumpling. The unprecedented economic growth made some feudal lords so rich and so powerful that they demanded more political power. Princes who were supposed to rule different states of the great kingdom under a centralized Zhou court started to dream of more autonomy and greater territory. Some assumed the position of *ba* 霸, feudal leader, and was able to control other states and discharge many of the functions formerly performed by the Kings, and made the Kings nothing more than bearers of the title. Later, the states began to wage wars against each other (the "Warring States" period, 403-221 B.C.E.). The Zhou ritual system was undergoing disintegration, and the society was witnessing deep moral decline, social chaos, and general destruction. It was upon such a historical background that China had its most glorious period in philosophy. The greatest minds of China—Confucius, Lao Zi 老子, Mo Zi 墨子, Zhuang Zi 莊子, Mencius 孟子, Xun Zi 荀子, Han Fei Zi 韓非子, to name just a few, were all born during that time. It was the age in which the foundation of the Chinese intellectual heritage was laid, perfectly comparable to what Greek philosophy did for the Western civilization.

Intellectually, Confucius had few books to rely upon and had no school to go to for his own education. The mysterious book, *Yi Jing* (*I Ching* 易經, *Book of Change*), was still basically a book of divination; its profound philosophical significance was yet to be revealed, interpreted, and articulated. Other literatures in poetry, history, and music etc. were also in their primordial form, awaiting to be edited, commented, or even documented. The philosopher had to fully exercise his ingenuity, insights, and creativity to formulate his own theory, and he did that amazingly well. What he provided were not only answers to the immediate social crisis, but something much more fundamental. He addressed questions about value, about the world and human life in general, as we shall see in the subsequent chapters.

The Life of Confucius

Confucius was born in Qufu, a town in the state of Lu in central China, known for its preservation of the early Zhou rituals and music. His family name is Kong 孔, and his given name Qiu 丘. "Confucius" is a Latinized term for "Kong Fu-zi 孔夫子," which literally means "Master Kong" in Chinese. His father, a military officer, died when he was only three years old, and his mother, from whom he received his primary education, raised him in a relatively humble situation.

Confucius spent his life mainly on four mutually integrated kinds of activities: learning, teaching, editing ancient classics, and offering political services.

His heart was set upon learning at the age of fifteen, and he was ever since a determined learner for his entire life. He learned from the classics that he edited. According to today's classification, they ranged from philosophy, literature, history, music, to social sciences. He also learned from the people that he encountered. "Walking in a company of three, I will surely find a teacher [among them]," says the Master. "Selecting out their good points, I follow them; identifying their faults, I improve myself accordingly" (7/22). He learned also from traveling around, visiting historical sites, and experiencing life. Entering the Grand Temple, he inquired about everything. Upon climbing the Eastern Mount, he started to see how small the State of Lu was, and upon ascending the Mount Tai, he came to the realization that the world underneath was not big either (see Mencius, 7A/24). It was a realization with profound significance,

5

comparable to Plato's allegory of the cave—One's vision is dependent on how high one stands.

Confucius is considered China's first teacher, though it depends clearly on how the word "teacher" is defined. Before Confucius, education did exist, but it was given mostly to a person in a tutoring fashion, usually from parents to their children, governmental officials to their subordinates, masters to their disciples. Confucius was probably the first to offer systematic education in an institutional way, the first to make teaching a career and an art, and the first to recognize the transforming power of education. He offered a comprehensive liberal education program, which consisted of "Six Arts"—ritual, music, archery, charioteering, writing, and arithmetic—to whoever wanted to learn and showed dedication by paying a moderate tuition. He defined the aim of education to be more than just the acquisition of knowledge, but more fundamentally a transformation of the person and preparation for public service. He began his teaching career in the thirties, and throughout his life, he had over three thousand students. Among them, seventy-two became conversant with the Six Arts.

Confucius considered himself a "transmitter" rather than a creator. The wisdom that he taught, according to himself, was already entailed in the ancient traditional rituals, the history, music, poetry, and the limited written works, which were, though corrupted in surviving the turmoil of the ages, still available at the time. He made researches into the rites of the Three Dynasties (Xia, Shang, and Zhou) and composed the *Book of Rites*. He selected and arranged according to historical order the recitals in the *Shu* 書, the *Book of History*. In ancient times the *Shi* 詩 was comprised of more than three thousand pieces. Confucius deleted the duplications and the fragments, and selected three hundred and five that exemplified the rites and righteousness, comprising the present *Book of Odes*. In his later years he was so fascinated by the *Yi Jing* (the *Book of Change*) that he read it repeatedly so much so that the leather strings which bound the book wore out three times. He edited, or might have authored the "Shi Yi, 十翼 (Ten Wings)," known as the Appendices to the text of the *Yi Jing* proper. The works done by Confucius were by no means merely technical. He was reconstructing, and in that sense, creating, with his vision, insights, and deep understanding, a set of canons that the later ages would have to follow. His own teachings were recorded by his students and collected in the book the *Analects*, which is commonly acknowledged to be the most reliable source of his theory.

Confucius considered public service a mission that he was obligated to conduct, as a practice of his philosophy, and as a way to implement his humanistic ideas into reality. In the early years he served as a keeper of grain stores and then in charge of the public shepherds. But his real political career began in his late forties and early fifties, when he was made the chief magistrate of a town, and set up a model administration. He became assistant minister of public works and, finally, the minister of justice in the state of Lu. His evident contribution to the peace and security of the state alerted a neighboring state. Feeling threatened by the rising power of Lu, the state bribed the ruler of Lu with eighty beautiful girl dancers and one hundred twenty fine horses to seduce the ruler to sensuous pleasures. Deeply disappointed with the ruler's indulgence in the pleasures, Confucius left Lu with some close disciples, in an attempt to find another state that would be interested in implementing his humanitarian ideas. In the following thirteen years of self-imposed exile, Confucius was sometimes driven away by the rulers to whom he did nothing but offered his best advice, and sometimes he had to refuse offers that required him to serve injustice. He survived some life-threatening situations, and finally returned to his home state Lu at the age of sixty-eight. His only son, Li, and his favorite disciple, Yan Hui 顏回, died in the year after his return. "Heaven has destroyed me, Heaven has destroyed me," sighed the Master (11/9). After spending the rest of his life teaching and editing, he died, at the age of seventy-three, with no anticipation of his subsequent fame.

A Brief History of Confucianism.

Due to the persistent effort of Confucius' followers, especially Mencius (390-305 B.C.E. a student of Confucius' grandson Zi Si 子思), and Xun Zi (325-238 B.C.E.), Confucianism became a major voice among the rival systems of thought. It is not incidental that Confucianism is known today as "The Way of Master Kong and Master Meng" in China. Mencius not only elaborated Confucius' teachings to greater details and followed Confucius footsteps to implement the ideas into governmental affairs, he contributed a great deal to the Confucian theory of human nature, the theory of *Qi* 氣 (vital energy), and the theory of a humanitarian government.

The first sweeping attack against Confucianism was from the First Emperor of the Qin 秦 Dynasty (reigned from 221-209 B.C.E.). Accepting the Legalist advises, the Emperor believed that laws had to be enforced with absolute authority, thoughts must be uniformed, and Confucian humanitarian ideas were harmful for his dictatorship. Confucian books were burned and Confucian scholars were buried alive. But the fact that his dynasty collapsed within a short period of time was a strong evidence of the validity of the Confucian humanistic ideas.

In the succeeding dynasty, Han, Confucianism became for the first time an officially recognized state ideology. An imperial school was set to study Confucian classics, and an enormous amount of Confucian scholars entered into governmental services. Confucius was enshrined everywhere in the kingdom as a sacred authority, and as the most honored man under Heaven.

Not surprisingly, dogmatic indoctrination of Confucianism and ill-intended endorsement of it as a way toward power and wealth accompanied the triumph. With the downfall of the Han Dynasty, Daoism and Buddhism became strong rivals to Confucianism. Both Daoism and Buddhism are comparatively more spiritual (at least apparently) and metaphysical than Confucianism. As a response to the challenge, the Song and Ming dynasties Confucians brought another upsurge of Confucianism by their creative interpretation of it metaphysically and spiritually, and thus inaugurated the "Second Epoch of Confucianism" (Tu Wei-ming).

The Western arrival in China around the nineteenth century and the decline of the Chinese political system triggered another major rejection of Confucianism. As Wm. Theodore de Bary says,

> In the paroxysms of revolution, and especially in the May Fourth Movement of 1919, which, as the great breaking point between old and new, is celebrated as the highest expression of the liberationist spirit, Confucianism was made to stand for all that was backward and benighted in China. It bore all the burden of the past, charged with innumerable sins of the old order.

Up to today, says de Bary, Confucianism is still used to justify the rulership "by a political elite," by "a party dictatorship allegedly for the people." The "dramatic appearance of the 'Goddess of Democracy' at T'ian-an-men," which is either "inspired by the Statue of Liberty (a French creation) or by the classic female impersonation of 'Liberté , Egalité et Fraternité '" would "least of all be identified with anything Chinese or with Confucian tradition" (de Bary, 103-8).

However, a rival voice is getting stronger. According to the leading advocators of Confucianism today (most of them live in the most economically and technologically advanced countries of the world), not only the evils should be attributed more appropriately to the abuses of Confucianism by intentional or unintentional misinterpretations of Confucius' teachings, to the contrary, Confucian philosophy is what we should count on for recovery from the materialized and alienated world and for the revitalization of humanity. A "Third Epoch of Confucianism" is approaching.

Why was Confucianism so influential? Why did it get such strikingly diverse evaluations? After all, what did Confucius teach? Whatever your final conclusion will be, I hope the following chapters will help you to reach your answer.

2

The Unity between Heaven and Human Being

Confucianism is often portrayed as a religion. That is fine if we define religion broadly. There is certainly a spiritual and religious dimension in Confucianism. It contains a strong sense of mission, a journey that is not supposed to end before death (8/7). What it aims at is even more important than life itself (15/9). But for those who conceive religion in a narrow sense, associated with worship of deity and institutionalized priesthood, the word "religion" can be quite misleading. There is neither deity worship nor priesthood in Confucianism. Confucian temples are more like monuments than monasteries. People go there for paying respect to the Master, and not for worship. In fact even the word "Confucianism" does not exist in China! Beside "the Way of Confucius and Mencius," which was mentioned in the last chapter, the word that Chinese people use for "Confucianism" is "*ru jia* 儒家"—The Ruist School. "*Ru*" refers not to Confucius. It refers to the theories and practices most distinctively represented by Confucius.

In what sense then, can Confucianism be considered religious? What is Confucius' attitude toward the Ultimate, eternity, and the meaning of life? These are the questions that this chapter will address.

This World vs. Other Worlds

Confucius' own attitude toward issues regarding deities and life after death is skeptical and pragmatic. "The Master did not talk about strange phenomena, ⋯ or spiritual beings" (7/21). His advice is to "Keep a distance from spiritual beings while showing them due reverence" (6/22). The reasons are indicated in the following passages:

> Zi Lu asked about serving spiritual beings, but the Master replied, "If you are not yet able to serve other people, how can you serve spiritual beings?" He then asked about death, but the Master replied, "If you do not yet understand life, how can you understand death?" (11/12)

> When the Master was gravely ill, Zi Lu asked if he might offer a prayer on his behalf. The Master queried, "Is this kind of thing ever done?" Zi Lu replied, "Yes, there is a eulogy that states: 'We pray for you the gods of Heaven and Earth.'" The Master said, "Then I have been praying myself for a long time." (7/35)

From these passages, it is evident that the Master did not conceal his lack of knowledge about matters related to spiritual beings or to life after death. He refrained from speculating or conjecturing things that he had no knowledge about. Just like Lao Zi, the founder of Daoism, who said in the *Dao De Jing* 道德經, "To know that you do not know is knowledge" (chapter 71), and like Socrates, who is well known for his motto, "Knowing one's own ignorance is wisdom," Confucius said, "To say you know when you know, and to say you do not when you do not. That is knowledge" (2/17).

Confucius did not reject the possibility that there might be spiritual beings, and he took the possible deities respectfully.

> When Confucius offered sacrifice to his ancestors, he did it as if his ancestral spirits were actually present. When he offered sacrifice to other spiritual beings, he did it as if the other spiritual beings were actually present. He said, "If I am not fully present in the sacrifice, it is no different from having no sacrifice at all." (3/12)

Confucius believes that we have a closer responsibility for serving

11

the people in this world, and serving the people in this world should be the best way for getting blessings from spiritual beings, if there are any. It is in this sense he had been "praying" for a long time. For him, if one lives according to the Decree of Heaven, whether or not there is a life after death and whether or not there are spirits will not matter, for there will be nothing to be regretted. Once Zi Gong asked Confucius whether those who were dead had consciousness, the Master said, "When you die, you will eventually know. It will not be too late to know by then" (*Shuo Yuan* 説苑 "Bian Wu 辨物," see Sun & Guo, 21). When asked about whether it would be better to be on good terms with the god of the kitchen rather than with the spirits of the shrine, the Master said "No. Those who commit sins against Heaven have no god to pray to" (3/13).

Immanence vs. Transcendence

One of the gravest misunderstandings of Confucianism is to take the Confucius notion of Heaven (*tian* 天) to be transcendental, in a way the Christian God is, separated from the world in which we live and through which our destiny is explained or determined but not vise versa. Inherited from the early Zhou, the Confucian notion of Heaven is immanent to the world. In replacing the Shang Dynasty notion of *Shang Di* 上帝, "Lord-on-High," with the notion of Heaven, the Western Zhou predecessors gradually depersonalized the "Lord" without losing its sense of being a reality that governs worldly affairs, and they brought the being from on high down to the Earth where people actually live. Human beings began to be seen as a part of Heaven. The will of Heaven was no longer the will of an anthropomorphic deity that issues orders and gives blessings and sanctions from above; it immanently exhibited itself in popular consensus and in regular patterns of discernible social and natural events, and it could be affected by the moral undertakings of the people. Under such a notion, rulers were considered sacred only so long as they were able to remain entrusted by the Mandate of Heaven (*tian ming* 天命).

The *Book of History* (*Shang Shu* 尚書) has such a passage: "Heaven sees through the eyes of the people, Heaven listens through the ears of the people." Even though the passage is unmistakably anthropomorphic, what is anthropomorphic is actually the anthropogenic. Heaven here is virtually embodied in the people and exemplified by the people. A philosopher from the British Empiricist tradition would tend to take "people" in this passage to be merely organs through which Heaven receives its sense data, but it is definitely more plausible to interpret the passage to be commonsensical, uncontaminated by the Empiricist distinction between sensing and judging.

That the will of Heaven is displayed through patterns of social and natural events can readily be seen from the following saying of Confucius:

> Does Heaven speak? And yet the four seasons turn and the myriad things are born and grow within it. (17/19)

Heaven in this passage is a principle according to which natural events take place. The same philosophical implication is in the *Book of Change*. The divination based on reading the pattern on tortoise shells after they are heated and yellow stalks after they are scattered entails the belief that everything in the universe is governed by the same principle, whether in an intentional or purely naturalistic way.

The *Book of Change* also entails the view that humans can affect their destiny through their own activities. It tells people not only what situation they are facing, but also what kind of action should be taken given the specific situation. People of Western Zhou believed that what affects Heaven most effectively is moral undertakings, especially those by the ruler. A song from the *Book of Odes* demonstrates the mentality clearly:

> The Mandate of Heaven,
> How beautiful and unceasing!
> Oh, how glorious
> Was the purity of King Wen's virtue!
> With blessings he overwhelms us.
> We will receive the blessings.
> They are a great favor from our King Wen.
> May his descendants hold fast to them. (Chan, 6)

Heaven and human are in a special kind of part-whole relation. Hall and Ames point out that there are different kinds of part-whole relations. A part can simply be a constituent of the whole, as in the case of an apple being part of a bag of apples. A part can be a functionally interrelated element of the whole, as in the case of a stomach being part of a digestive system. A part can be a particular instance of a universal archetype, as a particular chair is an instance of chair. The kind which applies to Confucian Heaven-human relation is one in which a part reflects, contains, and affects its whole, as in the case of the hologram (Hall and Ames, 237-8). They used the Hua Yan Buddhist analogy of a hall of

13

mirrors to illustrate the point. In a hall that is full of nothing but mirrors, every mirror reflects all the other mirrors, and is in turn reflected by all the other mirrors. A part in this kind of part-whole relation both defines and is defined by the whole. Humans in the Confucian conception are such parts of Heaven. To each individual, his relationships with others around him are the channels through which he is able to affect and is affected by others. So far as the individual represents the relationships, the individual is the condensed whole, and the whole exhibits itself through the individual. So far as the individual affects and is affected by his surroundings, he is not identical to the whole; the whole is something beyond, though not detached from, the individual.

Of course, it does not mean that everyone can affect the whole to an equal degree. Those who are in certain positions can affect the whole more than others do. But at the same time, one's own effort is also a determinant. The fact that Confucius, a person born in humble circumstances, was able to affect Chinese history and civilization more than any Emperor did, is a clear demonstration. Confucius' most famous successors Mencius and Xun Zi both said that everyone is capable of becoming a sage king, and characteristically all Confucians feel that the Decree of Heaven is bestowed on them.

Anxiety vs. Curiosity

The realization that human conduct can affect the will of Heaven logically leads to the sense of being responsible for one's own destiny. This realization, says the contemporary Confucian Xu Fuguan 徐復觀, is the root of the whole Chinese philosophical tradition. Greek culture started from a sense of curiosity or a motivation to know the natural world. For the Greeks, knowing was a leisurely activity for the sake of knowing itself, rationality was considered the defining feature of a human being, and the love of wisdom or contemplation was taken to be the source of happiness. These characteristics of the Greek culture resulted in the development of metaphysics, science, and technology as a manipulative power. To the contrary, the entire Chinese traditional culture is based on "*you huan yi shi* 憂患意識"—a sense of anxiety, which is a key linkage that runs all the way through Confucius, Mencius, Lao Zi, Zhuang Zi, Song and Ming Neo-Confucianism and even the Sinicized Buddhism (Xu, 1991, 176).

The biggest difference between the sense of anxiety and the

sense of dread and despair is that the sense of anxiety
originates from a person's vision obtained through deep
thinking and reflection about good fortune and bad fortune,
success and failure. The vision entails the discovery of a close
interdependence between the fortunes and the person's own
conduct and his responsibility to his conduct. Anxiety is the
psychological state of a person when his feeling of
responsibility urges him to overcome certain difficulties, and
he has not got through them yet. ··· In a religious atmosphere
centered on faith, a person relies on faith for salvation. He
hands all the responsibilities to God, and will therefore have
no anxiety. His confidence is his trust in God. Only when one
takes over the responsibility oneself will he have a sense of
anxiety. This sense of anxiety entails a strong will and a spirit
of self-reliance. (Xu, 1963, chpt. 2)

A result of the sense of anxiety is '*jing* 敬'—reverence. It is
different from religious piety in that

Religious piety is a state of the mind when one dissolves one's
own subjectivity and throws oneself entirely in front of God,
and takes refuge thoroughly in God. The reverence of the early
Zhou is a humanitarian spirit. The spirit collects itself from
relaxation to concentration; it dissolves bodily desires in front
of one's own [moral] responsibility, and manifests the
rationality and autonomy of the subject. (Xu, 1963, chpt. 2)

Because of this primary motivation, Confucian teachings are all
centered around two inseparable aims—the cultivation of oneself and
the manifestation of virtue to affect the world—both are about real life,
about value, with no purely theoretical interest in obtaining objective
knowledge about the natural world (Xu, 1952).

The point was further elaborated by Mou Zongsan 牟宗三, another
20th century Confucian. "The sense of anxiety," says Mou, "may quite
well be used to contrast with the Christian idea of the sense of guilt in
original sin and the Buddhist idea of suffering and impermanence." For
Christians, "original sin is a deep abyss of fear, the shore of the abyss is
salvation, and the refuge of the salvation is Heaven, to be close to God.
Heaven is the final refuge originated from the Christian idea of original
sin." For Buddhists, "the idea of suffering can be seen from the Four
Noble Truths. ···Sufferings caused by impermanence and frustrations

caused by craving form an abyss of suffering. Its salvation…is to take refuge in the tranquil realm of Nirvana." The Chinese sense of anxiety is different. It was

> not generated from original sin or the suffering of human life. It originated from a positive moral conscience, an anxiety over not having one's moral quality cultivated and not having learned. It is a sense of responsibility. What it led to were ideas such as reverence, the respect for morality, the manifestation of moral character, and the Decree of Heaven. (Mou, 13)

Heart-mind vs. the Intellect

Confucius says: "At the age of fifty, I knew the Decree of Heaven (*tian ming* 天命)" (2/4).

Because Heaven is immanent, it is possible for humans to know its Decree. Confucius did not explain specifically how he came to know the Decree of Heaven, but from his cautious attitude toward gods and spirits and life after death, we can assume that he used the word "know" quite seriously and honestly. We can also tell that it took him a long journey before he was able to know the Decree of Heaven, for he started his pursuit at the age of fifteen, and it was thirty five years later when he came to know the Decree of Heaven. We can further observe that the journey was clearly not one of logical reasoning, for otherwise he would have explained it to his disciples. It must be something that had to be experienced directly, and could not be explained fully by words. The assumption that knowing is the awareness of a certain proposition's being true, and therefore knowledge must be explicable in words, had never existed in the Chinese philosophical tradition. This knowledge of the Decree of Heaven was the result of the Master's direct experience, most likely from introspection of his own *xin* 心, "the governing part of the self," that both feels and thinks, perceives and makes decisions. The word is translated quite properly as "heart-mind," since the English word "mind" alone would be too intellectual, and the word "heart" by itself would be too emotional.

It was after the age of fifty—the age that he came to know the Decree of Heaven—Confucius made the following remarks, when he encountered two personal dangers, once from a man named Huan Tui in the state of Song who tried to kill him by felling a tree, and another from the people of Kuang, who attacked him for they thought that he was an enemy whom Confucius resembled in appearance.

> Heaven has bestowed virtue in me. What can Huan Tui do to me? (7/23)
>
> Since the death of King Wen, is not the course of culture (*wen* 文) in my keeping? If it had been the will of Heaven to destroy this culture, it would not have been given to a mortal [like me]. But if it is the will of Heaven that this culture should not perish, what can the people of Kuang do to me? (9/5)

The confidence manifested in these sayings is clearly derived from the realization that he embodied the virtue or the culture that King Wen used to represent, which was believed to be the Decree of Heaven that enabled King Wen to overthrow the Shang Dynasty. Unmistakably there was a faith in the power of the Decree of Heaven by which he believed that virtue was going to prevail. But the faith was not a reliance on an external deity. It was in the power of the virtue itself which he embodied. Again, Xu Fuguan's remarks are appropriate:

> According to traditional religious beliefs, Heaven issues commands to humans from without, from above, and humans, as the subjects of their own life, are in a passive and inactive state. Yet to Confucius, Heaven shows up in one's own nature, and the requirements from Heaven become the requirements of the nature of the subject himself. (Xu, 1963, chpt. 4)

Typically Mencius is credited for establishing a theory of human nature for Confucianism. Indeed Confucius' disciples did not hear the Master talk about his own view about "nature" (5/12). The only occurrence of the word "[human] nature" in the entire *Analects* is in 17/2: "Humans are similar in their nature. Through practice they become far apart." Another citation only faintly suggests that Confucius believed the in-born goodness of human nature: "Humans are born straightforward"(6/19). Such a ground is less than adequate for us to say that Mencius' theory of the goodness of human nature was already implicit in Confucius' own teachings. There are even passages in the *Analects* that suggest the opposite. Confucius said: "I have yet to see people who are truly fond of *ren* [benevolence, or human-heartedness], and abhor the contrary" (4/6), and "I have yet to meet a person who is fond of virtue more than of physical beauty" (9/18). The Master was obviously more confident about his own virtue than about others'. He did not make it clear whether he was born with the virtue or he acquired it through learning. But clearly he took the virtue as the Decree of Heaven, and felt a strong sense of mission, of responsibility, of reverence and awe towards it. Here moral feeling and religious feeling became one.

It was Mencius who clearly pointed out that every human being is born with incipient moral tendencies—the "Four Hearts"—the heart of compassion, the heart of shame, the heart of courtesy and modesty, and the heart of right and wrong (Mencius, 2A/6, 6A/10). Those tendencies are what differentiate us from beasts, and therefore are what human nature consist of and where the Decree of Heaven resides.

Decision vs. Discovery

Confucius and Mencius did not merely discover the Decree of Heaven in them through their introspective experience of the moral tendency. It was also their choice, their decision, and their act of affirmation to recognize the humanistic tendencies to be the Decree of Heaven.

As anyone familiar with the Western philosophical tradition knows, there is a big "is" and "ought" problem in moral philosophy. Simply finding that there are moral tendencies inside (which is about what *is* the case) does not mean that it is the Mandate of Heaven, much less than one must live according to it (which is about what *ought* to be the case). When one engages in the process of retrospection, one may find sympathy in others' sufferings, a sense of shame in accepting intimidating treatments, etc., but one also finds other tendencies in the heart-mind, such as the craving for possession, for pleasure, and for fame. To affirm the moral goodness, rather than the other tendencies of the heart-mind, to be the Decree of Heaven, is a decision, an act of affirmation, and a recommendation. The tension between these two aspects (discovery and decision) is evident in the following passage from *Mencius*, where Mencius tells us clearly that his affirmation of what is human nature entails a choice with practical consideration in it:

> It is due to our nature that our mouths desire sweet taste, that our eyes desire beautiful colors, that our ears desire pleasant sounds, …. But there is also fate (*ming* 命) [whether these

desires are satisfied or not]. The superior man does not say
they are man's nature [and insist on satisfying them]. The
virtue of humanity in the relationship between father and son,
the virtue of righteousness in the relationship between ruler
and minister, ·····—these are [endowed in people in various
degrees] according to fate. But there is also man's nature. The
superior man does not [refrain from practicing them and] say
they are matters of fate. (7B/24)

By emphasizing the inborn goodness in human heart-mind,
Mencius performed an action in declaring that he recognized that
particular part of us as the defining feature of being human. Mencius
says on the one hand that "man have the Four Hearts just as they have
their four limbs," and on the other hand, that one who is devoid of these
incipient good tendencies "is not a human" (2A/6). These two sides
show clearly that this theory about human nature is more stipulative
than descriptive. It is descriptive because it is a matter about fact
whether people do have those incipient tendencies or not. The question
about whether we are born with them, have a natural agreeable feeling
toward them, or we are conditioned by social norms created arbitrary to
accept them in the first place, and gradually internalized them as habits
afterwards, is to be answered by appealing to experiences. Yet it is
stipulative because after all, if our experience *does* find exceptions, we
should say that the people who are devoid of the tendencies are not
genuinely human, instead of modifying the description and say, "most
people, not every human being, have the tendencies." Here experience
is no longer relevant for justifying the thesis. The matter becomes one
of stipulative definition, and that is dependent upon one's subjective
choice and decision.

The choice of affirming what is moral to be the Decree of Heaven
underlies Confucius' entire life. In learning, he selected good points to
follow, and identified faults to improve himself accordingly (7/22). In
educating his students, he did not merely help them to discover who
they actually were. He helped them to transform themselves into higher
levels of moral and aesthetic perfection. In political life, he did not
complain about Heaven (14/35), even though Heaven often appeared to
be at odds with him. The Master believes that

It is the human being who is able to make the Way great, not
the Way that can make the human being great. (15/29)

19

In editing books, he chose only the poems that exemplified ritual propriety and righteousness for the *Book of Odes*. He mixed his moral judgements in *Spring and Autumn*, a history book, and differentiated the right from wrong, good from evil. Consequently religious judgement was substituted with historical judgement—By putting the good and the evil deeds all into the historical record for people to praise or condemn, the good received their reward and the evil received their punishment. The mentality of the nobles ever since was that they were more afraid of the judgement of the history than the judgement of the gods. Later, the famous Han Dynasty historian Sima Qian 司馬遷 continued the work. Motivated by establishing morality and orienting the history, Sima Qian made great contributions to the establishment of the Confucian moral authority.

One thing that has to be made clear is that our use of the words "choice" and "decision" is in a "modest" sense, as Professor Joel Kupperman calls it. According to Kupperman's analysis, it is the sense in which we can even say we choose not to run naked through a session in a philosophy conference, or choose not to torture a child to death. In a more restricted sense of the words, however, we do not choose or decide in those kinds of matters. For most of us, our moral characters would have ruled them out as real options before they even came to our minds, even though they are still, speaking from the modest sense, within our capacity to do and up to us to choose. For Confucius and Mencius, their choice of taking the Way might very well not be "real" choices, because they had cultivated themselves to such a level of perfection that other options would not even occur in their minds. Their ideal was also to make people, themselves included, of course, to that level of perfection so that one may simply act out of her "second nature" on those important moral matters without the need to make choices in the restricted sense of the term (see Kupperman, 102-114).

Decree of Heaven vs. Fate

Besides the notions of Heaven (*tian*) and the Decree of Heaven (*tian ming*), Confucius sometimes talked about *ming*, a term usually translated as "destiny" or "fate." Since the word for decree or mandate is also the same character *ming*, and it is even used in some cases as an abbreviation of *tian ming*, the Decree of Heaven, it is easy to confuse the two. The distinctions and relationships between the three become quite complicated and even controversial, and yet the issue is of philosophical importance. Here I would like to clarify them a little bit according to what would be the least controversial, and then proceed to explain the Confucian view about *ming*.

From what has been said in the previous sections, it should be clear that not everything from Heaven is its Decree. The Decree is discovered and decided by the moral agent him or herself. The word "*ming*" is used mainly to mean something close to destiny, though as Hall and Ames point out, we should carefully guard against any hint of transcendence that may be carried over by the word, i.e. that things destined are predetermined or fixed beforehand (Hall & Ames, 213). *Ming* is different from the Decree of Heaven in that the latter is more of a moral imperative, and the former is more of a determination of certain phenomena, usually in a particular order or sequence. For instance, when a natural event happens beyond a person's control, it would be considered *ming*.

> Bo Niu was ill. Confucius went to look in on him. Grasping his hand through the window, he lamented, "It is due to the *ming* that we are losing this man. That such a man could have such an illness! That such a man could have such an illness!" (6/10)

Similarly, whether the Way eventually will prevail or not, given the human efforts involved, is determined by *ming* (14/36). Whether or not a person will end up having a long life, wealth, and high social status, given the person's own way of conducting his life, is also a matter of *ming* (12/5). In those cases, "*ming*" is interchangeable with "*tian*," Heaven.

Those passages show that Confucius fully recognizes the fact that humans do not have full control of everything, even though we can make differences within a certain limit. The relationship between what is and what is not within our control is well explained by Mencius:

> Though nothing happens that is not due to destiny [*ming*], one accepts willingly only what is one's proper destiny. That is why he who understands destiny does not stand under a wall on the verge of collapse. He who dies after having done his best in following the Way dies according to his proper destiny. It is never anyone's proper destiny to die in fetters. (Mencius, 7A/2)

Mencius also quotes the *Book of Odes* to illustrate the point:

> By always studious to be in harmony with destiny, and rely on your own efforts, you will get much happiness. (2A/4)

21

The picture is clearly not fatalistic. The Confucians never thought that everything was predetermined and that no human effort would make any difference. To the contrary, they believed that, though there is always a limit to what a human can do, humans should never complain about Heaven. Instead, they should rely on themselves to make a difference.

Only when a man invites insult will others insult him. Only when a family invites destruction will others destroy it. Only when a state invites invasion will others invade it. The Tai Jia [from the *Book of History*] says: When Heaven sends down calamities, there is hope of weathering them; When man brings them upon himself, there is no hope of escape. (Mencius, 4A/8)

This is where the notion of *ming* 命 can be close to the Decree of Heaven, for human beings take part in both. What one perceives to be the Decree of Heaven will affect one's destiny. The following story is an interesting illustration:

Sima Niu lamented, "Everyone has brothers except me." Zi Xia said to him: "Life and death are a matter of destiny; Wealth and honor lie with Heaven. The exemplary person is deferential and faultless, respectful of others and refined, and everyone in the world is his brother. Why would the exemplary person worry about not having brothers?" (12/5)

By redefining what it means to have brothers according to the Decree of Heaven, namely to be a morally exemplary person, Sima Niu should be able to gain control of his own *ming*—destiny. In that case he would be *ming*ing his *ming*. The story coincidentally illustrates another important point of the *Analects*, namely the role of "names:"

Zi Lu asked Confucius, "If the lord of Wei was waiting for you to bring order to his state, to what would you give first priority?" Confucius replied, "Without question it would be to order names properly. ...When names are not properly ordered, what is said is not attuned; when what is said is not attuned, things will not be done successfully; when things are not done successfully, the use of ritual action and music will not prevail; when the use of ritual action and music does not

22

prevail, the application of laws and punishments will not be on the mark; and when laws and punishments are not on the mark, the people will not know what to do with themselves." (13/3)

Needless to say, the method of correcting names has a limited range of effectiveness. When the Decree of Heaven is apparently in conflict with destiny, Confucius' attitude is to follow the former. That is why he is considered "a man who does what he knows to be impossible" (14/38). Here again, we see a religious conviction of Confucius.

Contextual Person vs. Atomistic Individual

No understanding of the Confucian account of the unity between Heaven and human can be complete without articulating the contextual perspective of Confucianism.

According to a Western individualistic notion of human being, a person is an autonomous choice maker and falls only incidentally into some specific relationships with others. This atomistic notion of human being never occurred in Confucius' mind. For a Confucian, one's specific relationships are part of what the person is. Detached from the context of relationships, the person is merely an abstraction. As Henry Rosemont puts it,

> For the early Confucians there can be no me in isolation, to be considered abstractly: I am the totality of roles I live in relation to specific others. Moreover, these roles are interconnected in that the relations in which I stand to some people affect directly the relations in which I stand with others, to the extent that it would be misleading to say that I 'play' or 'perform' these roles; on the contrary, for Confucius I am my roles. (Rosemont, 72)

Just think about ourselves: Besides being a son or daughter of our parents, a brother or sister of our brothers and sisters, a friend of our friends, a neighbor of our neighbors, etc., in a word, abstracted from the roles one has in social relations, what is left over would be nothing but a biological being. When we make choices, we do not choose as a solitary individual. The parameter of our choices will be defined by and affected by the people we have specific relationships with, and the outcome will in turn affect these people. Even if you decide to go to a nobody's land and start an entirely new life, you would be a person who deserts everyone—in that case you are still defined by your relationship with others.

The notion of a contextual human being is reflected broadly in how traditionally Chinese people conceive themselves. It is no coincidence that Chinese put their family name first and their "first name" last. The fact signifies that they conceive themselves first of all a member of the family and then, only secondary, themselves as individuals. Even the "first names" of siblings often show contiguity or relatedness. My three brothers and I, for example, have one of the four Chinese characters, "*zhong hua ren min*" 中華人民, meaning "Chinese People," in each of our first names, in the order of our age. My father-in-law and his siblings' first names are, again in the order of their age, "*ren*," "*yi*," "*li*," "*zhi*," "*xin*," 仁義禮智信, the "five Confucian virtues"—human-heartedness, righteousness, ritual propriety, wisdom, and trust-worthiness. The way that Chinese write a mailing address also indicates their mentality of identifying individuals through the community to which they belong—it starts with the largest vicinity necessary for identifying the location, down to the more and more specifics. For example, sending a letter abroad, the Chinese writes the country first, then the province or state, the city, the street and number, and finally the name of the individual receiver.

Out of this contextual notion of human being and the notion of immanent Heaven, as we explicated in the preceding sections, the Confucians never felt that the lack of personal immortality would lead to the lack of meaning for life, for their life may go infinitely beyond the narrow biological span. A very common application of this broad notion of immortality is the continuation of the family line, which Confucians also honor. Among the things that are considered bad to do to one's parents, the worst is to have no heir, says Mencius (Mencius, 4A/26). Another bad thing to do to one's parents is to behave immorally and to make the parents ashamed of him. Both of these "bad things" done to parents need to be understood beyond the parents' own immediate personal state, and enter into the way they "exist" in others. The fact that Chinese people take how others will look at them very seriously, and that they expect their children to bring honor to the family and the community to which they belong, are clear indications of their conception of themselves. Their existence extends to the heart-minds of other people. Confucius' saying that "If for three years [of mourning] one does not change from the way of his father, he may be

24

called filial" (1/11) can also be understood from this light, for that is a way for the father to continue to be "alive."

The best illustration of this notion of immortality is a conversation that took place when Confucius was still a child (546 B.C.E.), which established a standard for the Chinese in the ensuring 2500 years to follow. When Fan Xuan Zi of the State of Jing asked Mu Shu, an officer from Confucius' home State, Lu, what the ancient saying "Dead but immortal" meant, and whether it was correct to interpret it as unbroken heritage of the family bestowment, Mu Shu replied:

> According to what I have heard, this is called hereditary rank and emolument, not immortality. There was a former great officer of Lu by the name of Zhang Wen-chung. After his death his words remain established. This is what the ancient saying means. I have heard that the best course is to establish virtue, the next best is to establish achievement, and still the next best is to establish words. When these are not abandoned with time, it may be called immortality. As to the preservation of the family name and bestowment of membership in the clan branch in order to preserve ancestral sacrifices uninterrupted from age to age, no state is without these practices. But even those with great emolument cannot be said to be immortal. (Chan, 13)

The establishments of virtue, of achievement, and of words, are known as "Three Immortalities." Confucius' endorsement of the idea is displayed in some passages of the *Analects*. One of them is, "Exemplary persons despise the thought of ending their days without having established name" (15/20). From the context of his overall teachings, the "name" clearly referred to the three achievements mentioned above, particularly the first. Another passage suggests the same:

> Duke Jing of Qi had a thousand teams of horses, and on the day he died, the common people had nothing out of which to praise him. On the other hand, Bo Yi and Shu Qi died of starvation at the foot of Shouyang mountain, and the common people praise them down to the present day. Is this not what it means? (16/12)

What is common to the Three Immortalities is that, first of all,

25

they are all relational—the immortalities are not achieved through personal survival of death, but through continued existence and manifestation of the person's efficacy in the community and in the history. Secondly, they are all beneficial to others. It is not that through immoral behavior one cannot achieve immortality. One Chinese saying, often used to characterize "bad guys," goes, "If he cannot leave a good fame for hundreds of years, he wouldn't mind leaving a notorious reputation for the ten thousand years to come." The reason that all the "Three Immortalities" are morally beneficial ones is that they are the ways to achieve the unity between Heaven and human being. Indeed, how can there be a real unity without being harmonious?

Obviously this kind of immortality, or the unity between Heaven and human, is neither guaranteed nor dependent on the mercy of a deity, nor achievable through solitary effort. One needs to pursue it in one's own course of life within the community, which is what we will get into in the following chapters.

3

Ren—Human-heartedness

The word "*ren* 仁" appears in the *Analects* 105 times, and fifty-eight of the 499 sections in the book are devoted to the discussion of the concept. No any other concept has such a prominent place in Confucius' philosophy.[1] Yet Confucius never offered a precise definition of the concept himself, nor were translators able to come up with a unified English translation. The concept of *ren* seems to be an ideal that even the Master himself claimed never to have fully reached (7/34), and yet it is so close to everyone that the Master says, "Is *ren* far away? No sooner do I seek it than it has arrived" (7/30). One of the Confucian classics, The *Doctrine of the Mean*,[2] has a line that is expressive of the paradox:

> There is nothing more visible than what is hidden and nothing more manifest than what is subtle. (chpt. 1)

What is *ren* then?

The Nature of *Ren*

"*Ren*" has been translated as "benevolence," "human-heartedness," "authoritative person," "altruism," "humanity," "goodness," etc. While all the translations capture the meaning of the term in one way or another, a good understanding of the concept has to be based on more than reading the translations.

Let us first make some observations about the word and its usage in the Confucian texts.

One observation is that the word "*ren*" is sometimes used in Confucian texts to be somewhat synonymous to "human" or "person," which is homophonic to it—*ren* 人 (see Mencius, 1B/15 and *Doctrine of the Mean* 20). Hall and Ames reason from this fact that

> it follows that the distinction between the two terms [人 and 仁] must be qualitative: two distinguishable degrees of what it means to be a person. This same kind of distinction is captured in the familiar kind of expression: "There are persons and there are *persons*." (Hall & Ames, 114)

It is true in both English and Chinese that the word "person" or "human" sometimes carry moral implications. Expressions like "That person is a beast with a human skin," "One should really be like a human," "A human should be treated like a human," are within the common stock of Chinese expressions. They indicate that there are certain moral decencies expected for being a human. For this reason the word "*ren*" can be interpreted as a quality that makes a person an authentic human being, which every biological person needs to strive toward.

A second observation is the fact that the word is made up of two elements, one is "person 人" and the other the number "two 二." Ames and Rosemont point out that

> This etymological analysis underscores the Confucian assumption that one cannot become a person by oneself—we are, from our inchoate beginnings, irreducibly social. (Ames & Rosemont, 48)

Indeed, many descriptions of *ren* that Confucius offered were about interpersonal relations. "*Ren*" is to "love the people"(12/22), says the Master, and the method to be *ren* is "*shu* 恕"—comparing one's own heart with other hearts with compassion (6/30). This is an obvious endorsement for the necessity of having a community in the heart-mind of the *ren* person. Mencius also characterizes the heart of compassion to be the root of *ren* (6A/6), and compassion presupposes the "other" that one is

28

compassionate to. This analysis is also consistent with the contextual feature of the Confucian concept of person that I explained in chapter two.

A third observation is from the textual analysis of the *Analects*—Confucius gave different answers to different disciples, even when they asked the same question about *ren*. Pedagogically that was to point out different dimensions of *ren* to each disciple according to the particular aspect in which the disciple lacked adequate grasp. But it indicates also that *ren* defies any attempt to capture it fully in a concise fixed definition or formula. It is more like an art that needs to be mastered and embodied with the entire person, and to be displayed in one's gestures and manners, rather than a formula to be understood or accepted by the intellect.

From what has been said so far, it is fair to say that *ren* means a quality that has to be achieved and fully embodied before a biological person can become an authentic human being. For the lack of a better word, I shall adopt the translation "human-heartedness," as long as it is not taken to be merely a psychological state that comes and goes. The word is general enough for different manifestations of the quality, and it seems to capture the genuine humanness more than other words do.[3]

The "Golden Rule"

Twice when asked about *ren*, Confucius answers

Do not impose upon others what you yourself do not want. (12/2, 15/24)

This is called the negative version of the "Golden Rule," for it tells people what *not* to do. The more commonly known version of the "Golden Rule" in the West is the positive one—"Do to others as you want others to do to you." Some scholars wondered why Confucius gave the negative version only, and they tried to find reasons by comparing it with the positive version. However, Confucius did endorse a positive version also, for he says:

If you want to establish yourself, establish others. If you want to promote yourself, promote others. (6/30)

The "Rule" is considered "Golden" because it seems to capture what is moral at a substantial level, and can be considered a general rule of

29

conduct to which all the other rules would follow. It is indeed so universally endorsed that various versions of it are found in all the major religions in the world.

It must be stressed that even though Confucius taught the "Golden Rule," he never took it as a rule, much less a "Golden Rule." He states clearly that a morally exemplary person (*jun zi* 君子) "is never for or against anything invariably. He is always on the side of the right" (4/10). Confucius "rejects ... inflexibility and rigidity" (9/4). "The morally exemplary person is devoted to principle but not inflexible" (15/37). Confucius himself was, as Mencius characterized him, a sage who acted according to circumstances, rather than according to rules (Mencius, 5B/1). The art of flexibility is deemed by the Master so high that he says,

A man good enough as a partner in one's studies may not be good enough as a partner in the pursuit of the Way; a man good enough as a partner in the pursuit of the Way may not be good enough as a partner in taking a stand; a man good enough as a partner in taking a stand may not be good enough as a partner in the exercise of *quan* 權. (9:30)

The word "*quan*" originally means "scale," and thus the action of "scaling" as well. According to *Gong Yang Zhuan* 公羊傳, a Chinese classic dated probably as early as Zhou Dynasty, "*quan* means moral goodness resulting from transgressing well-established classics" ("The Eleventh Year of the Duke of Heng"). To *quan* is to scale the circumstances and decide that, in a given situation, it is morally good or proper to take expediency, and to temporarily overstep a norm or principle.

The reason why the "Golden Rule" cannot be taken as a rule is not difficult to see. First of all, the "rule" itself is based on a person's likes and dislikes, and is therefore making whatever desires and wants one happens to have the criteria of morality. For a person who likes to be bribed, the Golden Rule would not only permit him to bribe others; it would obligate him to do so. Secondly, the rule also assumes that all human beings are alike and that what we want for ourselves is good for others as well. A person who likes others to quarrel or intrigue with him all the time would be obligated by the rule to quarrel or intrigue with others all the time, whether they like it or not. A *roué* who would want some young woman to climb into his bed at night would be justified in climbing into her bed at night (Gewirth, 133-4). The negative version of the Golden Rule is equally subject to counter-examples. Kant says, in commenting on the "Golden Rule," that "the criminal would on this ground be able to dispute with the judges who punish him" (Kant, 37, note 23). For if the judges themselves do not like to be punished, then according to the rule they should not impose onto others what they themselves do not desire. Similarly,

> the collection of money owned by recalcitrant borrowers, the payment of lesser wages for inferior work, the giving of lower grades to poorer students, and the infliction of many similar sorts of hardships would be prohibited by the Golden Rule whenever it could be shown that the respective agents would not themselves want to undergo such adverse treatment. (Gewirth, 134)

It is evident that the "rule" works only under the condition that the person who uses it is qualified to judge rights and wrongs in the first place and would not simply infer from whatever desires and impulses he himself happens to have. Confucius is not at all uncritical about one's desires and wants. In fact one of Confucius' major descriptions of *jen* is "To restrain the self" (12/1). For Confucius, cultivating one's heart-mind is almost a life-long journey. He says that he himself did not reach the state where he can follow his heart's desire without overstepping the line up until the age of seventy (2/4). This message implies that he had to regulate his desires so that he would not overstep the line of morality until he has no desires that will urge him to overstep it. He would be self-contradictory had he believed that the "Golden Rule," hence the influence from one's desires and wants, should be the criterion of morality and be observed absolutely. Indeed, it follows also that for Confucius, the "Golden Rule" cannot be a rule at all. A rule should be able to take an indefinite variety of decision-types as inputs and deliver in each case one option—or set of options—as output, as the most appropriate option. The "Golden Rule" cannot guarantee such an output, and the appropriate application of the "rule" itself is dependent upon an independent criterion for right and wrong.

"Shu"—A Method to Be *Ren*

How should we take the Confucian "Golden Rule," if it is not meant to be a rule at all? Confucius has given us an answer in the contexts where the statements of the "Golden Rule" are found. One of the passages, quoted completely, is:

> Zi Gong asked, "Is there one expression that can be acted upon throughout one's entire life?" The Master replied, "There is *shu* 恕. Do not impose on others what you yourself do not want." (15/24)

In another passage, right after the statement of his positive version of the "Golden Rule," the master says:

> Taking an analogy near at hand is the method of becoming human-hearted (*ren*). (6/30)

The word "*shu*" consists of two parts, the upper part is "*ru* 如," which means "like," "as if," "resemble," and the lower part, "*xin* 心," means "heart-mind." This etymological analysis helps us to understand that for Confucius, the application of the "Golden Rule" is to take one's own heart as an analogy near at hand, and to extend one's considerations to the wants and needs of others by comparing one's own heart-mind with others' in a compassionate and empathic way. According to such a reading, the "Golden Rule" is no different from "*shu*," a *method* to be *ren*.

As a method, the "Golden Rule" can help us to discern rights and wrongs, and decide what is the right thing to do. Even though there is no guarantee for the right action, the method can at least take people close to what is right in most scenarios. A method is different from a rule. A rule is *imposed upon* the agent, such as a master's order has to be obeyed by his servant. Even in the case of self-imposed rules, the subject that obeys the rules feels obligated to follow the rules. A rule, by its very nature, is to *disable* the agent from doing certain things, and it allows no exceptions or violations. A method, on the other hand, is *mastered* by the agent in the way that an artistic skill is mastered by an artist. The agent fully embodies the method, not merely being aware of it and understands it. It *enables* the agent to perform the right action and it permits exceptions when situations demand some other method.

As a method, *shu* or the "Golden Rule" is more importantly a way of becoming a human-hearted person, a genuine human being. By exercising *shu*, the person will become sensitive to the presence of others, and mind their interests whenever an action is going to affect more than the agent herself. The Master ultimately aims not at providing a formula for people to make right moral decisions accordingly, but at making persons who are able to "*quan*" (scale the circumstances) with their own cultivated heart-mind, and ultimately be in no need to make "real" decisions. The right action will be for them as natural as water's running down the stream and balloon's going up to the sky.

Furthermore, the above two points should not be taken separately. The person cannot develop a human heart-mind independently of its applications. It is somewhat like learning a native language, through apparently discrete instructions and particular applications, one grows into it. Even the ones who teach a native language—primarily the parents—do not know how to describe the language itself independently of its applications. The learning-teaching process is very complicated and even mysterious, yet it goes on commonly in everyday life, and has always been amazingly successful. Children develop the ability of telling the difference between appropriate and inappropriate applications of ordinary expressions at a very young age, though formal education is necessary for more sophisticated uses. Their ability may go well beyond those who lack practical encounter with other speakers of the language, yet otherwise well-learned in the rules of grammar. Similarly, it is difficult (if not impossible) to describe human-heartedness apart from how it manifests in life. Even if one were able to define human-heartedness verbally, the method of *shu* can be more effective for moral education than offering verbal definitions. Most people who are able to determine whether it is moral, say, to quarrel with another or to jump into another's bed simply because one wants the other to do the same to oneself, would not be able to specify their own criterion for such a judgement; yet they have no problem in seeing that in those cases, the "Golden Rule" does not apply.

Love the People

Another major description of *ren* offered by Confucius is to "Love the people" (12/22).

This notion of "love" is similar to the one used in the Christian *Bible,* "You shall love your neighbor as yourself" ("Leviticus" 19:18, "Matthew" 19:19 and 22:39, "Mark" 12:31, "Romans" 13:9, "James" 2:8). It means love in the sense of caring and respecting, not in the sense of natural affection. Natural affections between parents and children, between different sexes are not the kind of love that differentiates humans from animals. But on the other hand it is different from a sense of moral duty. The love must be out of the heart, not merely out of the rational faculty of the mind. It is a cultivated spontaneity, fully embodied in the *ren* person. Kant might say that actions have moral worth only in so far as they are done out of the sense of moral duty, not from inclinations. The actions done out of inclination may be in accord with what moral duty requires the person to do, but they are consequences of the inclinations, in a way like natural events are caused by preceding events. They can be very nice, but have nothing to do with morality. The Confucian distinction between a biological person and an authentic person (a *ren* person) would defy the dichotomy between either out of moral duty or out of natural inclinations, and show the moral worth of actions done out of the cultivated spontaneity. The person who, as a consequence of cultivating her moral virtues, does what moral duty requires her to do with a strong inclination to do it, and does it pleasantly. This kind of action deserves more moral credit than those done merely out of the sense of duty without the genuine heart behind it. For the latter kind is not from a cultivated person, and the motivation for the action is therefore not fully embodied, but rather resides in the "practical reason" only. The former, however, deserves the credit because the action is done out of the fully embodied virtue which the agent has acquired through her own diligent cultivation.

Extending beyond personal interest and into interpersonal caring, love is characteristic to human-heartedness. It is a natural outcome of *shu*, comparing one's own heart-mind with others' with compassion and empathy. One of the four things that the Master abstains from is being self-absorbed (9/4). Whether in daily life or in governmental affairs, a *ren* person is always considerate and has others' interests in mind. In running a government, the *ren* ruler "is frugal in his expenditures and loves his subordinates, and puts the common people to work only at the proper season of year" (1/5). Those are minimum requirements for a ruler. If the ruler is able to "be broadly generous with the people and is able to benefit the multitude," it would be even better than *ren*, and should be considered a sage (6/30). In daily life, an exemplary person "loves the multitude broadly" (1/6). She "does not explore others' fondness of her, nor does she exhaust others' kindness to her" (*Book of Rites*, chpt. 1). She "does not intimidate others by showing off her own talent, nor belittle others by revealing their shortcomings" (*Book of Rites*, chpt. 32). These are also among the requirements for being an authentic person. A sage is one who can live in this way consistently throughout life, and apply the human-heartedness broadly to everyone.

Just like the "Golden Rule," love by itself does not guarantee that what it dictates is always morally right. According to Confucius, love should be given in a right way. When Confucius' favorite disciple Yan Yuan died, other disciples gave Yan Yuan a lavish burial despite the Master's warning that it would not be proper. Confucius was very upset (See 11/11). In this case, Confucius' feeling upset was because of love, for he could not have let Yan Yuan be treated in a proper way. But his

34

disciples' conduct was also out of love. Clearly, according to Confucius there is a difference between proper and improper ways of love, and a proper way of love is that it be given in accordance to what is right. One may disagree with Confucius about what is proper in this particular case, but it is not at all difficult for anyone to find cases in which a person acts out of love and does immoral things to the loved ones, such as violating the loved one's rights; nor is it difficult to find cases in which a person cares for the well-being of another but ends up making the person miserable.

One of the qualifications for a proper love is to love with distinction or differentiation. First, Confucius differentiates according to relationships and social roles. "When his stables caught fire, the Master hurried back from court and asked, 'Was anyone hurt?' He did not inquire after the horses" (10/17). It does not mean that he cared nothing about animals. "The Master fished with a line, but did not use a net; he used an arrow and line, but did not shoot at roosting birds" (7/27). It means that he puts the caring for human peers prior to his caring for animals. Among humans, he also believes that one should treat each other according to their relationships and social roles. "The ruler should be treated as a ruler, the subject a subject, the father a father, the son a son" (12/11).[4] While one should extend one's love as broadly as possible, Confucius believes that one must start with the love of one's own parents, and gradually extend to others according to degrees of closeness in relations. This order is the very fabric of an ideal Confucian society.

Secondly, he differentiates according to circumstances. He would rather help the needy than make the rich richer (6/4). If the rich are his own parents and the needy are strangers, he would help the strangers, provided that his own parents are well cared for.

Thirdly, the Master differentiates according to moral integrity.

> Zi Gong said, "Do exemplary persons have things they detest?"
> "They do indeed," said the Master. "They detest those who announce what is detestable in others; they detest those subordinates who would malign their superiors; they detest those who are bold yet do not observe ritual propriety; they detest those who, being determined to get what they want, are unrelenting. But Zi Gong, don't you, too, have things you detest?" Zi Gong replied, "I detest those who pry out matters for the substance of wisdom; I detest those who think that immodesty is courage; I detest those who think that revealing the secrets of others is being truthful." (17/24)

To those with ill will, the Master repays them with uprightness rather than kindness. If you repay ill will with kindness, says the Master, "then how would you repay kindness" (14/34)? It is thought provoking to compare this as a third option in addition to the dichotomy between "eye for an eye and tooth for a tooth" on the one hand, and Jesus Christ's exhortation to turn the other cheek, on the other hand.

Love with or without distinction was a major disagreement between Confucians and the Moists. Mo Zi 墨子 (470?-391? B.C.E.), the founder of Moism, advocated universal love without discrimination. Of the arguments from the Confucians against Moism, the following four stand out to be the strongest.

First of all, it is not natural to love without distinction. Confucius' following remark applies beyond its immediate reference: "Sacrificing to ancestral spirits other than one's own is being unctuous" (2/24). While it is perfectly natural, though gracious, if one offers kindness to someone who is related in some way or is in need for the kindness, it is insinuating if the kindness were distributed universally, regardless.

Secondly, it is not right to love without distinction, for it implies the denial of one's own father; and the denial of one's own father is to be no different from beasts, says Mencius (Mencius, 3B/9). When a father or mother is loved and cared for no more than any stranger, not only the very basis of family relationship collapses, and consequently, the order that is vital to social harmony will no longer exist, humans will lose the moral superiority that differentiates them from animals. For the Confucians, we owe our parents our life and the care and love we received from them when we were young and could not care for ourselves. The love and care provided us not only the material needs, but also what we had to have in order to grow into a decent human being. A person who grows up without being cared for or loved would be dramatically different from a normal human, and his or her personality would be very twisted. A human being should be enormously grateful to their parents and pay the parents the due love and care that they deserve. A point made by Scottish philosopher Thomas Reid may help us to see this point. It is a self-evident principle in morals, says Reid, that "unmerited generosity should yield to gratitude" (Reid, 639).

Thirdly, it is often impossible to love without distinction. Imagine that one wants to send a New Year 's greeting card to someone. According to the principle of love without distinction, one has to send the card to everyone in the world. Since this is simply impossible, the person, in order to remain faithful to the principle, has to send the card to no one. In some cases, love without distinction seems to be possible if one knows how to do it properly. When the administration of the state of Zheng was in his hands, Zi Chan used his own carriage to take people across the rivers,

> "He was a generous man," commented Mencius, "but he did not know how to govern. If the footbridges are built by the eleventh month of the year and the carriage bridges by the twelfth month, the people will not suffer the hardship of fording. An exemplary person, when he governs properly, can clear the path for people when he goes his way. How can he find the time to take each person across the rivers? Hence if a governor is to please every one separately, he will find the day not long enough." (Mencius, 4B/2)

But even in this case, it is impossible for Zi Chan to build bridges for all the people in the entire world; and in building the bridges, it is impossible for him to build them all at once, without some priority.

Fourthly, from the consideration of moral education, it is advisable to work from the "root."

> The morally exemplary person concentrates his efforts on the root; for the root having taken hold, the Way will grow therefrom. Aren't filial piety and fraternal deference the roots of becoming human-hearted indeed? (1/2)

Here again, we find the love to be both a characteristic of the *ren* person and a method of becoming *ren*. By practicing *ren*, *ren* grows. If we do not start our love from the immediate context of our life, and with those who we immediately encounter, it will not start at all.

It must be stressed that the Confucians are not saying that one should not love all. It is rather that love should be given in proportion to several considerations stated above, and when possible, be extended as far as one can, with priority given accordingly. As Mencius puts it:

> Treat the aged of your own family in a manner befitting their venerable age and extend this treatment to the aged of other families; treat your own young in a manner befitting their tender age and extend this to the young of other families, and you can roll the Empire on your palm. (Mencius, 1A/7)

Respectfulness, Reverence, and Leniency

When asked about *ren*, the Master also at different times characterized it with some important moral virtues, for instance, respectfulness (*gong* 恭), reverence (*jing* 敬), leniency (*kuan* 寬), beneficence (*hui* 惠), quick in action (*ming* 敏), doing one's very best (*zhong* 忠), reliability in words (*xin* 信), and slow to speak (*yan ren* 言訒) (17/6, 13/19, 12/3). In this section, we shall discuss the first three.

In the *Analects*, the word "respectfulness" (*gong*) usually applies to humans, mainly to oneself, as in 16/10, "to appearing respectful when it comes to demeanor" (see also 15/5). The word "reverence" (*jing*) applies both to humans, usually other than oneself, and to business or public affairs, as in 2/20, "How can one inculcate in the common people the virtue of reverence, of doing their best?" and in 16/10, "to being reverent when performing duties."[5]

Kant is well known for his view that humans are ends in themselves, i.e. they have unconditional value. That is because as rational beings, humans can make free choices and choices are the source of all the values. Confucius also values humans, but for different reasons. For Confucius, one earns reverence from others by being respectful oneself. "If one is respectful, one will not suffer insult"(17/6, 1/13). Confucius says, "The exemplary person does not speak more than what he can accomplish, and does not behave across the line of proper conduct, people revere him without being forced to" (*Book of Rites*, chpt. 27). This view is fully in line with the view that what makes a person authentic is *ren*, human-heartedness. Without *ren*, one does not deserve the due reverence for a human being.

The above contrast between Confucius and Kant can be spelled out in the following five important differences: First, the Kantian ethics advocate *universality* of the worth of a human being, based on rationality, the Confucian ethics advocate *particularity* of the worth of a human being based on moral cultivation. Secondly, while rationality itself provides only the *possibility* of being moral, Confucius requires the *actuality*, or the actual effort of becoming moral. Thirdly, for Kant, respecting a human being is a moral imperative *dictated* by the reason, and one does not have to embody the reverence fully. Confucius requires the reverence to be fully *embodied*—the person to be revered must have respectfulness, and the people who revere must have the feeling from their heart, not from their brain. Fourthly, the Kantian respect for humans is an *imperative*, whereas the Confucian respect is both a *method* and a *consequence* of cultivation. Finally, Kantian respect for humans aims at laying the ground of universal imperatives for *everyone* to follow, Confucian respectfulness and reverence, while also intended to be for everyone, aims more at *one's own* cultivation and conduct.

Repeatedly Confucius reminds his students to set strict standards for themselves and to be lenient (*kuan*) to others.

> If one sets strict standards for oneself and makes allowance for others, he won't likely to be complained about. (15/15)
>
> Do not worry over not having an official position; worry about what it takes to have one. Do not worry that no one acknowledges you; seek what will qualify you to be acknowledged. (4/14, see also 14/30, 15/19)
>
> Exemplary persons make demands on themselves, while petty persons make demands on others. (15/21)

In this sense, the Confucian learning is "for improving oneself"(14/24). The sage kings of the antiquity used to say, "If I transgress, let not the ten-thousand states be implicated; if any of the ten-thousand states transgresses, the guilt is mine" (20/1). What we see here is much more than merely a leniency to others. It is double edged: The leniency to others is at the same time strictness to the self. It implies self-reliance, a strong sense of responsibility and confidence of the self. The exemplary person digs the source of energy and power from within, and she turns her sense of "anxiety" into a moral courage, a driving force to improve herself, and through which, to benefit all. If she has done her very best and the circumstance does not let her have a success, she would have ease in her mind, for she knows that she has tried her best and did all she can do.

Confucius did not say that we should just mind our own responsibility and tolerate whatever others do. Leniency is somewhat like the "principle of charity" in scholarship. When it comes to interpreting others, one gives the best interpretation, and when it comes to the examination of one's own work, one should allow no room for mistakes or misinterpretations. Leniency does not mean to have no criticisms or objections against other's wrong ideas or behaviors. In dealing with others' faults, says the Master, "Attack depravity itself rather than the person who depraves" (12/21). Do not be like the petty persons who "In employing others, demand all-round perfection" (13/25). "Do not level blame against what is long gone" (3/21).

Beneficence

The exemplary person will not be content with merely perfecting herself, but will actively seek to benefit all, including herself. She or he "gives the common people those benefits that will really be beneficial to them," and is therefore "beneficial but not extravagant" (20/2). Being beneficial is the manifestation of the human-heartedness.

What about the Master's saying that "The exemplary person is persuaded by what is right, and the petty minded person is persuaded by what is profitable" (4/16)? How would Confucius respond to a Utilitarian, who believes that the right thing to do is that which will maximize utility, which usually translates as happiness? And how would Confucius comment on Kant's distinction between hypothetical and categorical imperatives, the view that separates utility motivated actions and morally motivated actions entirely?

The answer is twofold: That human-heartedness is not in conflict with utility, to the contrary it is an effective way of bringing utility; and that when utility and morality are in conflict, being an authentic person regardless, is the way to resolve the conflict.

Let us first broaden the notion of utility beyond mere psychological feelings of happiness, and define it in terms of the overall well being of the person—the healthy state of a genuine human being, which includes both one's mental-psychological condition and the biophysical condition. Such a definition is necessary for us to understand the Confucian view about the inseparability of the mental and the physical, which we will bring up again in chapter six, but shall have to depend upon for elaboration of the present subject.

Confucius seldom talks about profit (*li* 利, see 9/1). This might be because that the common definition of the word is narrowly confined to material well beings. But his view that moral cultivation is a way of bringing benefit in a broad sense is clearly entailed in some of his sayings. For instance, in public affairs,

> If a person is proper in conduct, others will follow suit without need of command. But if the person is not proper in his own conduct, others will not follow even when they are commanded (13/6).

A more immediate personal benefit of being moral is indicated by the saying, "Those who are *ren* have longevity" (6/23). The reason for this is, explains the Han Dynasty Confucian Dong Zhong Shu 董仲舒 (179-104 B.C.E.),

> that they are not greedy of external things and they are tranquil and pure internally; their heart-mind is peaceful, harmonious, and is not out of balance. They nourish their person with the best things from Heaven and Earth." (Dong, chpt. "Xun Tian Zhi Dao 循天之道")

The explanation naturally refers us to another of the Master's answers to the question about *ren*: "To overcome the self and return to the observance of the ritual propriety" (12/1). Clearly, "overcome the self" should not be understood as merely a preach for ethical altruism. It is a method of self-care and self-perfection, including the health of the body. The Master says,

> There are three things against which an exemplary person is on his guard. In his youth, before his blood *qi* [spirit or vital energy] has settled down, he is on his guard against lust. Having reached his prime, when the blood *qi* has finally hardened, he is on his guard against strife. Having reached old age, when the blood *qi* is already decaying, he is on his guard against avarice. (16/7)

Guarding against one's own lust, strife, and avarice are clearly taken in this message as ways to protect one's essential well being.

Mencius elaborated the Confucian view in greater detail. Regarding governmental affairs, "It was by sharing their enjoyments with the common people the men of antiquity were able to enjoy themselves" (1A/2). The reciprocal relation justifies the government of *ren* (*ren zheng* 仁政).

> One who has the Way [of *ren*] will have many to support him; one who has not the Way will have few to support him. In extreme cases, the latter will find even his own flesh and blood turning against him while the former will have the whole Empire at his behest. (2B/1)

Similarly, regarding personal well being, to care for one's own person, "nothing is more effective than having fewer desires," says Mencius (6B/35). To summarize the point by an analogy, the one who searches for profit and yet not appeal to *ren* "is like looking for fish by climbing a tree" (Mencius, 1A/7, see also 4A/7).

Mencius further developed a theory of *qi* 氣 to be a metaphysical ground for the above view. "*Qi* [vital energy] is what pervades and animates the body," and "the will (*zhi* 志) is the leader of *qi*." "When the will is there, *qi* comes." But because the will is not merely an instant decision-maker, it depends on life long cultivation, *qi* does not come "at will," so to speak.

> It is produced by the accumulation of righteousness and cannot be appropriated by anyone through a sporadic show of rightness. Whenever one acts in a way that falls below the standard set in one's heart-mind, it will collapse. (Mencius 2A/2)

On the other hand, if the *qi* is properly nourished by righteousness, it can become so vast and unyielding that "it will fill the space between Heaven and Earth" (2A/2), and "the ten-thousand things will be here in me" (7A/4). I discussed in some detail somewhere else about the proper way of reading these sayings (see Ni, 1996 and 1999). The main points of my analysis are that the sayings are most likely based on real experiences accessible only to those who are morally well cultivated, often in their meditative state, and the sayings demonstrate the Confucian outlook of the universe—everything in the universe is interconnected in such a close way that they form a continuum, and the *qi* may be the media through which harmonious and friendly exchange of energy and information (for the lack of better words to articulate the contents of *qi*) between people and even objects can take place.

It should be made clear that for Confucius and his successor Mencius, morality is not an external boundary within which one can seek utility (such as the principle "Thou shall not lie" prohibits a doctor from lying to a patient), nor is it merely a favorable condition for utility (such as filial piety provides parents conditions to be cared for); it is the very cause of utility, or the very action that brings utility itself!

This intrinsic relation between morality and benefit is philosophically significant. In Kantian philosophy, moral imperatives ("ought") are dictated by practical reason, and are irrelevant to the kind of "ought" associated with matters of fact. "You should not lie" is different from "honesty is a good policy to gain people's trust." To evaluate the former, we use "right" or "wrong;" to the latter, we use "effective" or "ineffective." The former is a categorical imperative, which is about morality; the latter is a hypothetical imperative, which is a matter of strategy or technique. The Confucian view that morality can be a technique for bringing desired ends sounds like reducing moral imperatives to "hypothetical imperatives," which implies that if they were not effective, they could be discarded.

Neither Confucius nor Mencius left us with a direct answer to the question. But from what they taught, it seems that they would first question the dichotomy between categorical and hypothetical imperatives. There can be a third option: A moral imperative can be an effective means for benefit (a hypothetical imperative) only when it is taken categorically (absolute, unconditional). When King Hui of Liang asked Mencius how he would be able to profit his state, Mencius replied:

> What is the point of mentioning the word 'profit?' All that matters is that there should be *ren* and rightness (*yi* 義). ···If all those above and below are trying to profit at the expense of one another, the state will be imperiled. (Mencius, 1A/1)

Obviously Mencius is neither saying that profit is irrelevant to *ren* and *yi*, nor is he saying that *ren* and *yi* should be taken merely as a means for profit. He is saying that they are effective means for profit only when profit is not taken to be the end! This kind of view is also implied in Lao Zi's saying that "Because the sages are selfless, they attain self-fulfillment" (*Dao De Jing*, chpt. 7). The Buddhist morality pertains to the same insight. In order to reach Nirvana and freedom from suffering, one has to be moral (follow the Eightfold path); but if one were to become moral just for the sake of reaching Nirvana, one would defeat the very purpose, and can at the very best only avoid bad karma, and would not find the full enlightenment.

What is more unique to Confucians is that not only would they reject the dichotomy between categorical and hypothetical imperatives; their idea of the self is a unity between Heaven and human, a unity between the immediate person in the bodily form and the person who reaches universality through the community and eternity through the "Three Immortalities." In that sense, sacrificing one's life for the sake of moral principle can also be a way of pursuing one's own well being or perfection—a profit or utility in the broader sense that we defined earlier. When life and *ren* cannot be retained at the same time, sacrificing one's life for the sake of *ren* would be just like amputating a limb for the sake of saving one's life!

Looking from this perspective, it is perfectly understandable why Confucius and Mencius would say

> To eat coarse food, drink plain water, and pillow oneself on a bent arm—there is pleasure to be found in these things. The wealth and position gained through inappropriate means are to be like floating clouds. (7/16)

> Life is what I want; dutifulness is also what I want. If I cannot have both, I would rather take dutifulness than life. On the one hand, though life is what I want, there is something I want more than life. That is why I do not cling to life at all costs. On the other hand, though death is what I loathe, there is something I loathe more than death. That is why there are troubles I do not avoid. (Mencius, 6A/10)

Action and Words

Some important virtues of a *ren* person fit into this category: In practice, the *ren* person is quick (*ming*); in relationship with others, the *ren* person does his very best (*zhong*), and in speaking, the *ren* person is reliable in words (*xin*), and slow to speak (*yan ren*).

Quick in Practice

The virtue of *ming*, quick in action, is comparable to what Lao Zi said about how a wise person would respond to the insight of the Dao (the Way):

> The wise person, upon hearing of the Dao, practices it diligently. The average person, upon hearing of the Dao, takes it up now and then. The foolish person, upon hearing of the Dao, [would not only do nothing according to it, he] would laugh at it aloud. (*Dao De Jing*, chpt. 41)

44

The *ren* person is not satisfied with merely having an intellectual understanding. Actually according to Confucius, one cannot be *ren* without putting her understanding of *ren* into practice and letting herself be transformed and letting *ren* be manifested through her practice. It is through words and deeds the person reaches beyond the biological self and enters into communication with others; and also through this process, the person manifests her humanity and transforms herself to higher levels of perfection.

Confucius did not specifically discuss the "weakness of the will," i.e. the possibility of knowing what is good and, due to the lack of a strong will, fail to do what is good. Socrates is well known for his rejection of this possibility. Confucius, however, raised an interesting parallel question about the "weakness of strength." Is it possible that someone, who presumably knows what is *ren* and wants to practice it, yet lacks the strength to obtain it and act in accord with it?

> Ran Qiu said, "It is not that I do not rejoice in the Way of the Master, but that I do not have the strength to walk it." The Master said, "Those who do not have the strength for it collapse somewhere along the way. But with you, you have drawn your own line before you start." (6/12)

> Are there people who, for the time of a single day, have given their full strength to *ren*? I have not come across such a person whose strength proves insufficient for the task. There might be such cases of insufficient strength, but I have not come across them. (4/6)

Neither of the passages quoted above rejects the possibility of the weakness of strength outright. Yet the tone is clearly negative towards it. If the problem of the people like Ran Qiu is not the lack of *strength*, what is it? Is it that they actually lack the *knowledge* of the goodness of *ren*? Or is it that, albeit their knowledge of *ren*, they lack the strong *will* to practice according to it?

What is clear is that according to the Master, if one knows about *ren* and determines to embrace it, one has at least the strength to start the journey and will be quick in action to practice it.

A professional philosopher today often lives his life in a split way. In his profession, he speculates, reasons, and writes about things that have little to do with practical life. Away from his desk, his life has little to do with what he does in his profession. To a Confucian, however, his philosophy is his way of life, and he lives philosophically.

45

Confucius was a practical man who cared deeply about real life and was not merely interested in formulating a theory. Of course he was not good at doing everything. In farming, he was not as good as a farmer; in growing vegetables, he was not as good as a gardener (13/4). What he was particularly good at was cultivating the person and bringing social order and peace to the world. He was a "farmer" and a "gardener" in a different sense. "The various craftsmen stay in their shops so that they may master their trades; exemplary persons study so that they might promote the Way" (19/7). It is not that other kinds of activities have no worth.

> Even along byways, there are bound to be worthwhile things to see. The reason that exemplary persons do not pay attention to such things is because they have a long way to go and are afraid of being bogged down. (19/4)

The analogy is appropriate only in a limited sense. In fact the Way is not to be pursued in separation from one's professional life. How can one be a craftsperson and yet at the same time not be a son or a daughter, a father or mother, a friend, a colleague, a business partner, a member of the community, etc.? In handling one's own profession, can one not be at the same time handling human relations and displaying oneself as a person? The Way unfolds exactly in one's own handling of all these affairs in life, not in isolation from them.

Thus the *ren* person will

> be filial at home, and be deferential in the community, be cautious in deeds and be trustworthy in words, love the multitude broadly and be intimate with human-hearted persons. If in so behaving he still has energy left, he would use it to study literature. (1/6)

Indeed, if a person is able to do well in those regards, even if he is not schooled, he can surely be considered well-educated (1/7).

Slow to Speak

"An exemplary person wants to be slow to speak yet quick in action" (4/24). The reason that the person is slow to speak is that "claims made immodestly are difficult to live up to" (14/20), and "an

46

exemplary person is ashamed of letting their words go beyond what they can accomplish" (14/27). So "they first accomplish what they are going to say, and only then say it" (2/13).

Modesty as a virtue became characteristic to Chinese tradition due to the strong influence of Confucianism. Not only does the traditional Chinese person speak humbly and modestly about herself, she would decline praises that she fully deserves. This often puzzles Americans who do not understand the Chinese culture. "Are you saying that I was not speaking the truth when I praised you?" "Do you mean that the excellent banquet that you just hosted me with is your kind of 'nothing but an ordinary meal?'" What was actually meant by the Chinese person is, however, that "I should not feel proud of my accomplishment; I should instead always think about how to improve myself;" "you are such an honored guest that you deserve even a better treatment."

Doing One's Best

The meaning of the word "*zhong* 忠" in modern Chinese language is mainly "be loyal to." Indeed, it has been taken in this way for a long time. Rulers in imperial China took it in this way to demand unconditional obedience and devotion from their subjects. However, the word originally meant that in practicing what is right, one should do one's best, wholeheartedly. "Be not weary over daily routines, and take actions at one's best wholeheartedly (*zhong*)," says Confucius (12/14). It does not mean unconditional obedience. In fact, doing one's best requires that sometimes one has to oppose to whom one is serving.

> The Master said, "Can you really love someone without urging the person on? Can you do your utmost (*zhong*) for someone without instructing him?" (14/7)

When the ruler deviates from what is right, one way to do the very best for him is to "take a stand against him without duplicity" (14/22), and when that is obviously not going to do any good, "take to the high seas on a raft" as an overseas dissident (5/7) is another.

Trustworthy in Words

"A man not trustworthy in words (*xin* 信) is like a cart without a pin in the yoke-bar," says Confucius (2/22). This is on the same line with the Biblical Commandment "Thou shall not lie," as it is generally understood, which also includes keeping promises, seeing one's actions through to the end, etc.

However, Confucius does not take the virtue mechanically. "A man who insists on keeping his word and seeing his actions through to the end has a stubborn petty-mind," says the Master (13/20). Mencius also said that "a great man needs not necessarily keeping his word nor does he necessarily see his action through to the end. He aims only at what is right" (Mencius, 4B/11). The Confucians are not contradicting themselves. For the Confucians, being trustworthy is an overall consistency between words and action, not a rigid imperative taken at its face value. In some cases, to tell the truth or even just remain silent would be morally inappropriate. Suppose the Confucian's grandmother is dying and she asks him how does she look, the Confucian would not choose to say the truth "You look terrible!" nor would he give a silent response. He would, like most of us would, I believe, tell her a good-willed lie—"You look fine." In like manner, we do not abruptly decline a gift that we don't like.

The *Analects* have an interesting story about Confucius:

> Ru Bei sought to meet with Confucius. Confucius declined to see him, feigning illness. Just as the envoy conveying the message had stepped out of the door, Confucius took his lute and sang, making sure that the messenger heard it. (17/20)

Ru Bei is, apparently, a person to whom Confucius wanted to teach a moral lesson by making him feel ashamed of himself. However, Confucius did not refuse to see him directly, presumably because that would be an improper way to treat a visitor, or because that it would be too harsh to embarrass the person publicly. Confucius used a lie (that he was ill) to save the person's face publicly, yet at the same time, gave him the lesson by making him aware that he was rejected. Kant maintains that lying is to disrespect the ones who are lied to, and is therefore morally impermissible. Yet the Confucian story seems to suggest that the polarization of respect and disrespect, lie and being truthful, is again questionable. The way Confucius handled the case was both with respect and with disrespect, lying and being truthful.

Of course the exercise of this kind of art is not easy, and the flexibility of the principle can be misused as excuses for inappropriate maneuvers. Since Confucius could not tell people exactly when and where one can rightfully make a false statement, it is then practically left to every individual to decide as one sees fit. As a consequence, the people influenced by Confucianism have less hesitation in making an untruthful statement than the people influenced by Christianity, even when the lie is not clearly necessary. We may presumably blame Confucius for not having set the principle as a rigid rule, but the fault is more in the interpreters than in the Master; for the Master has instructed that the person is to be cultivated to embody and utilize the principle, and not that a principle should be forced upon the person who does not know how to use it properly.

Having said this much about *ren*, we should now make an important accretion to our working definition of *ren* formulated in the first section of this chapter—*Ren* is not only a quality that makes a person an authentic person; it is also a way toward a state of all round wellness, and an indication of an important part of the wellness itself. By "all round" we mean that the wellness is not merely in morality, nor even merely in mental health. It entails physical wellness and social (interpersonal) wellness also! To consider *ren* merely as a moral virtue that makes the person internally authentic is utterly inadequate. Only with such an awareness can we fully understand why the *ren* person will be quick in action and slow to speak, will do one's best, and will be reliable in words. As those qualities are more often seen in religious commitments than in philosophy, we see also from this awareness why Confucianism may be deemed as a religion and not a speculative philosophy.

---

¹ It is said that Confucius seldom talks about "*ren*," for the section 9/1 of the *Analects* apparently reads "The Master rarely spoke about advantage, and (*yu* 與) destiny, and (*yu* 與) *ren*." But that is obviously inconsistent with what the Master did. So I accept a less common interpretation of the word "*yu*" in the passage—instead of taking it to mean "and" I take it for "to endorse," "to give attention to," which is actually another meaning of the word.

² The *Doctrine of the Mean* was originally a chapter in the *Book of Rites*, and so was The *Great Learning*. Who the author of the two was is still uncertain. Some speculated that they might be written by Confucius' grand son, Zi Si, and yet others thought that they might have been composed by more than one author. They were both singled out and listed together with the *Analects* and *Mencius*, as the "Four Books" of Confucianism, by the Song Dynasty Confucian Zhu Xi 朱熹 (1130-1200).

³ Ames and Rosemont offer some good reasons for not translating the word "*ren*" in some other ways (see Ames and

49

Rosemont, 48-51). Their own translation of *ren* as "authoritative," however, seems to me less than satisfactory. Not only the word has an unfortunate association with the word "authoritarian," it is at its best able to capture only an extrinsic feature of the quality.

⁴ This passage has a double meaning. It also means that "The ruler must rule, the minister minister, the father father, and the son son."

⁵ See also 13/19, 15/6. Later, Mencius and his commentator Zhu Xi somehow reversed the two terms, making reverence (*jing*) a quality embodied by the agent and respectfulness (*gong*) the external exertion of reverence, and hence a quality of the action. See Mencius 4A/1.

4

Li—Ritual Propriety

Of Confucius' most outstanding followers, Mencius focused more on the notion of *ren*, Xun Zi focused more on the notion of *li* 禮, ritual propriety.[1] Which of the two followers is closer to Confucius' own teachings is an interesting scholarly issue. But the fact indicates that the importance of *li* in Confucianism is comparable to the notion of *ren*. In recent decades, the significance of *li* to philosophy and to human life in general is getting more and more recognition. Upon first reading, Confucius' emphasis on rituals, especially the details of rituals and their magical powers, seems irrelevant to us today. But upon reading him more carefully with the aid of recent developments in philosophy, says Fingarette, the same emphasis seemed to him one of the very aspects in which the Master was "ahead of our times" until recently (Fingarette, vii).

The Master said,

> In referring time and again to observing ritual propriety, how could I just be talking about the presence of jade and silk? (17/11)

What, then, was the Master talking about? To answer this, we must take a closer look at what the word means and how broadly and profoundly it exists and functions in human life.

The word *li* originally meant holy ritual or sacrificial ceremony,

51

and it was used by Confucius metaphorically to mean more broadly behavior patterns established and accepted as appropriate through the history by a community, including what we call rituals, manners, etiquette, ceremonies, customs, rules of propriety, etc. With such a broad notion, an enormous array of human activities can be included under this umbrella. The way we greet each other, a handshake, for instance, is ritualistic, for it is not a mere physical touch of hands. We stand up to greet our guests, and walk them to the door as they leave. Those are rituals, for merely speaking about efficiency they can be saved in most cases. We address people in a certain manner, though practically speaking, calling someone's attention can be done in many other ways. We even look at each other according to some implicit rules—at a very young age we start to know that it is impolite to stare at people, especially at certain parts of their body. We do things in appropriate settings. For instance a promise has to be made with the presence of the one who we promise to, for otherwise the mere utterance of the words does not count as a promise. In like fashion, a compliment or an excuse unheard is nothing. The list can go on infinitely, but for the present purpose it is adequate for us to see the point.

The metaphor of holy ritual serves as a reminder that the most ordinary activities that we do in our life can be ritualistic or ceremonial. It is from this metaphor the Confucian insights about our human life in the public space and time unfold.

Li as Embodiment of *Ren* and *Yi*

If we say that *ren* is the internal quality or disposition that makes a person an authentic person, then *li* is the body of external behavior patterns that allow *ren* to be applied and manifested publicly. "*Yi* 義," a word usually translated as "righteousness," is the appropriateness of actions. When *li* is properly performed, it is in accord with *yi*. Finally, the word "*dao* 道," usually translated as "the Way," means the course of taking the mission, or the mission itself. To use a metaphor, we may say that *ren* is the human heart-mind that is determined to travel onto the right road and the vision or sense of where the right direction is (be cautious not to take it merely as a psychological state, a feeling or a thought, for *ren* needs to be fully embodied), *yi* is the rightness of the road, and *li* is the way or manner in which one travels that allows the person to travel on the right road smoothly. The Way (*dao*), when used as a noun, is the right road itself, and when used as a verb, is to lead or

52

to head on to the right road in the right manner. The determination to travel on the right road and the knowledge of the right direction (*ren*) do not guarantee that the person will actually travel on the right road, nor will the rightness of the road (*yi*) guarantee that one will travel on the road smoothly and effectively. Likewise merely having *ren* does not guarantee that the *ren* person is able to live up to her ideal. The person needs to know *li*—ritual propriety, to be able to exercise her *ren* heart-mind properly and effectively.

The relationship between the notions can be further explicated by a pair of notions used by Confucius—"*wen* 文" and "*zhi* 質." *Zhi* means basic stuff, substance, inside principles, characters. *Wen* means the refined pattern, form, style, and outside appearance in which the *zhi* exists and unfolds. The relationship between the two is somewhat similar to the Aristotelian matter and form. For example, the cover and the pages of this book, the format of the typesetting, are *wen* of the content, while the content itself is the *zhi* of the refined form of the book. Yet in relation to the ideas that the content is trying to convey, the structure of the content, the language the author uses, are the *wen*, and the ideas themselves are the *zhi* of the content.

Now when the two notions are applied to appropriateness (*yi*) and ritual propriety (*li*), the Master says, "An exemplary person takes appropriateness as the substance [of his conduct], and carries it out in the form of ritual propriety" (15/18). Appropriateness is the substance (*zhi*) of ritual propriety, and ritual propriety the refined form (*wen*) of appropriateness. We may further use the notions to say that the conducts with both appropriateness and ritual propriety combined should be the refined form (*wen*) in which and through which a human-hearted person (*ren*) manifests her humanity.

Having clarified the relationships between the notions, it becomes obvious that *wen* and *zhi* should match each other.

> When there is a preponderance of *zhi* over *wen*, the result will be churlishness; when there is a preponderance of *wen* over *zhi*, the result will be pedantry. Only a well-balanced admixture of these two will result in an exemplary person. (6/18)

When someone said "Exemplary persons should focus on the substance, what do they need refined form for?" Confucius' disciple Zi Gong replied,

53

Refined form is no different from substance; substance is no different from refined form. The skin of a tiger or a leopard, shorn of hair, is no different from that of a dog or a sheep. (12/8)

The saying looks inconsistent with the Master's teaching, for the Master's saying which we have just quoted implies the possibility of having the two alienated from each other. But the point made by Zi Gong can be taken as a strong interpretation of the Master's teaching. According to this interpretation, the refined form and the substance of an exemplary person are so closely connected to each other that not only *should* they match each other; without one the other cannot exist! An appropriate conduct must have a refined form, otherwise it would not be appropriate; and a form cannot be considered refined unless it is appropriate. Similarly, one who does not do things in appropriate ritual forms cannot be said to be really human-hearted (*ren*), because there is no way that a real human-hearted would have no manifestation expressive of its content. On the other hand, real appropriate ritual conducts can only be found in those who are human-hearted, because an empty form will lose the beauty of its refinement.

The duality of form and substance, according to this strong interpretation, is not the relation between two entities. It is the relation between two inseparable aspects of the same thing. To borrow an analogy from the Zen Buddhist Master, Hui Neng 惠能 (638-713), the two are like the flame of a lamp and the light. When there is flame, there is light, and when there is light, there must be a flame. The value of the flame is in its radiation of light, and the light is emitted from the flame. One cannot reduce the ritual appropriateness displayed in public space and time back to an internal quality of *ren*, for that would suffocate the "flame" itself, nor can one abridge *ren* to its public manifestation, because the manifestation without that which manifests is a mere fiction. One limitation of this flame-light analogy though, is that it is one-directional. The flame radiates light but the light does not enhance the flame. In the case of *ren* and *li*, the practice of *li*, ritual propriety, is also a process of self-cultivation, of making the tradition one's own, and hence of making one *ren*. That is why when Yan Hui inquired about *ren*. The Master replied,

Through self-discipline and return to the observance of ritual propriety, one becomes *ren*. If for a single day one were able to accomplish this, the whole empire would defer to this model. (12/1)

It is no coincidence that in this saying, the inner cultivation (self-discipline) is listed together with the outer practice (return to the observance of ritual propriety).

As *ren* is the unique human quality that makes a person an authentic human, ritual propriety is a uniquely human way of behavior, and it is characteristic of human relationships at their most human.

> Zi You asked about filial conduct. The Master replied: "Those who are called filial today are considered so because they are able to provide for their parents. But even dogs and horses are given that much care. If you do not respect your parents, what is the difference?" (2/7)

By serving and dining with respect and appreciation, in a proper setting, the mere physical nourishment becomes a ceremony, and thereby becomes human. Learning rituals is therefore no different from learning to be a human, and the practice of rituals is the peculiarly human part of our life. Through ritual propriety, social activities are coordinated in a civilized way.

Now we can add one more specification to our explanation of the Confucian view of the human worth discussed in the last chapter—One needs to participate in the human ritual encounters in order to be an authentic human, and it is not possible to become an authentic human in solitude. There is a puzzling conversation in the *Analects*,

> Zi Gong inquired, "What do you think of me?" The Master said, "You are a vessel." Zi Gong asked, "What kind of vessel?" "A sacrificial vase of jade." (5/4)

In light of another saying, "Exemplary persons are not mere vessels" (2/12), the Master seemed to be telling Zi Gong that he was not a self-oriented and motivated authentic human yet. But why did the Master specifically compare Zi Gong to a sacrificial vessel? Fingarette's revealing interpretation is worth quoting in length:

> Such a vessel is holy, sacred. ⋯ Yet the vessel's sacredness does not reside in the preciousness of its bronze, in the beauty of its ornamentation, in the rarity of its jade or in the edibility

of the grain [that it contains]. Whence does its sacredness come? It is sacred not because it is useful or handsome but because it is a constitutive element in the ceremony. It is sacred by virtue of its participation in rite, in holy ceremony. In isolation from its role in the ceremony, the vessel is merely an expensive pot filled with grain. ... By analogy, Confucius may be taken to imply that the individual human being, too, has ultimate dignity, sacred dignity by virtue of his role in rite, in ceremony, in *li*. (Fingarette, 75)

However, the sacred vessel is still a vessel. An authentic human should not merely be *placed* in a ritual, one should *engage* in it. So the sacredness of a human is not merely being in the place, but being in the place as an active participant, who not only knows the intricate formality of the ceremony, but also has a well cultivated human heart-mind to manifest in the ceremony and to make the formality alive. The self-cultivation of the person is different from the preparation of the vessel. While the preparation of the vessel adds nothing but the beauty to be conferred for its sacredness in the ritual, the human-heartedness is where the sacredness and the life of the ceremony itself is derived from. In this sense, the Master might very well be telling the disciple that he still needed to cultivate himself in order to be more than just a vessel. It is typical that before a holy ritual takes place, the participant has to take a shower, fast for a certain period of time, and meditate for a while to calm down the mind and make the will sincere. If the placement alone would be enough to confer the holiness, all those processes would be unnecessary.

Though Confucius advocated the traditional ritual proprieties, no where did he say that they must be unchangeable. The Master said, for example,

> The use of a hemp cap is prescribed in the observance of ritual propriety. Nowadays, that a silk cap is used instead is a matter of frugality. I would follow the majority. A subject kowtowing on entering the hall is prescribed in the observance of ritual propriety. Nowadays that one kowtows only after ascending the hall is a matter of hubris. Although it goes contrary to the majority, I still kowtow on entering the hall. (9/3)

When asked about the root of observing ritual propriety, the Master replied,

What an important question! In observing ritual propriety, it is better to be modest than extravagant; in mourning, it is better to express real grief than to worry over formal details. (3/4)

The principle behind this is still the humanitarian spirit, *ren*, not the traditional formality (see also 11/1). Dehumanized formality was never Confucius' ideal.

Li as Fabrics of Social Order

Ritual proprieties often entail recognition of certain order. The time in which Confucius lived was a transition period when the old social orders were falling apart and social conflicts and turmoil became the norm of life. It was Confucius' vision to revive, reformulate, and thereby revitalize the traditional ritual proprieties, particularly those of the Zhou Dynasty, with humanitarian spirit, and to bring the society back into order. The fact that his home state, Lu, was richly endowed with that tradition was an advantage for him to obtain the vision, but he was not a mere traditionalist. His choice was well considered and innovative. By excavating the humanitarian spirit imbedded in the traditional ritual proprieties he found that the local culture had the potential of becoming an ideal universal principle of human society.

In the ideal Confucian society, "the ruler rules, the minister ministers, the father fathers, and the son sons" (12/11). Everyone knows his or her own social position, and conducts his or her life according to the rituals appropriate to one's specific position. The Master is himself a role model:

At court, when speaking with lower officials, he was congenial, and when speaking with higher officials, straightforward yet respectful. In the presence of his lord, he was reverent though composed. (10/2)

Here the rituals are the ways through which the social roles and relationships are confirmed and communicated, the responsibilities that come with them are taken, and the human-heartedness is displayed.

Later Confucians summarized human relationships into five kinds: ruler to subject, father to son, husband to wife, elder to younger brother, and friend to friend. Each pair is ordered with the

57

superordinate listed before the subordinate, except the last, which is equal unless some other differences become relevant. Those who are in superordinate positions enjoy more status of authority while bearing more responsibility, and those who are in subordinate positions enjoy more protection and less responsibility but are expected to return the former with respect and doing their best (*zhong*). This is the kind of social order that the imperial China relied upon. On a stone tablet elected in 1468 in the Confucius Temple at Qu Fu, Emperor Xian Zong of Ming Dynasty (明憲宗) wrote,

> Under Heaven, not one day can pass without the Way of Confucius. Why is this so? Because when the Way of Confucius is there, the social order is straight and the ethical principles are manifested; everything under Heaven is placed appropriately in their positions. Otherwise heresies will interfere and cults will arise. [If heresies interfere and cults arise,] how would the social order be set straight? How would the ethical principles be manifested? How would everything under Heaven be placed appropriately in its position? Therefore Confucianism is where the weal and woe of the people are dependent upon, and the peace and chaos of the state are contingent on. Those who rule the land under Heaven really cannot spare Confucianism even for just a single day.

But not all those in the ruling position were willing to acknowledge the Confucian view that, just like the polarity of *yin* and *yang* is not placid, people's social positions can change. To her husband the wife is *yin*, but to her son she is *yang*. When the son grows up and his parents old and vulnerable, the son may become *yang* and the parents *yin*. And finally the authority one enjoys at home is to a significant degree dependent on one's contribution to the family and one's moral integrity. One only has to recall two utmost cases to see the point—the fact that Confucius, a commoner at the beginning, was finally honored to be "Uncrowned King," to his symbolic statue even the Emperors would kneel down to pay reverence, and the fact that Confucius endorsed King Wen and Duke of Zhou, who overthrew their Emperor and became rulers themselves. A quote from Xun Zi made the point very clear:

> Yet although a man is the descendant of a king, duke, prefect or officer, if he does not observe the rituals (*li*) and

appropriateness (*yi*), he must be relegated to the common
ranks; although he is the descendent of a commoner, if he has
acquired learning, developed a good character, and is able to
observe the rituals and appropriateness, then elevate him to be
minister, prime minister, officer or prefect. (Xun Zi, 9)

One alternative way of bringing a social order is to use
administrative and law enforcement, which Confucius explicitly
denounced as inferior to the way of ritual propriety.

First of all, the administrative and law enforcement depends on
personal or institutionalized whim from above, with conscious efforts,
whereas ritual propriety is brought out from the bottom, within the very
society itself, for it is already there as a tradition. Once revitalized, it
requires little conscious effort to be effective. Furthermore, at that
particular historical era, it was unlikely that the rulers could sanction
anything but arbitrary and power driven orders, whereas the common
people's consensus, given the fact that most people at that time were
uneducated, was unable to take the lead. The tradition was readily there
to guide the people and provide the order. The rituals handed down by
the antiquity, especially from the Zhou Dynasty, was a repository of
past insights into morality, and as the insights were already actualized
in social custom, it was more than merely an intellectual heritage.

Second, the way of ritual propriety is more effective than the way
of administrative and law enforcement.

Lead the people with administrative injunctions and keep them
orderly with penal law, and they will stay out of trouble but
will have no sense of shame. Lead them with virtues (*de*) and
keep them orderly through observing ritual propriety and they
will develop a sense of shame, and moreover, will order
themselves. (2/3)

Compulsion and punishment can only ensure outward conformity, at
their best. People will be out of trouble not because they are ashamed
of doing wrong, but because they fear the punishment, and at places
where legal enforcement cannot reach or no one else is around to see,
they may still do wrong. However, if the social order is secured by
virtue and ritual proprieties, an internal supervision will develop, which
is much more effective in its penetration into people's lives, and the
ritual propriety can become social custom, saturated as a way of life
itself. The Master said,

In hearing litigation, I am no different from anyone else. But if you insist on a difference, it is that I try to get people to have no need to resort to litigation in the first place. (12/13)

Third, not only is the way more effective and practical in securing an order, it is a kind of order totally different from what law and administrative enforcement can achieve. The kind of order that Confucius envisioned is both more penetrating and less coercive in terms of its restrictive function; and more importantly, in addition to being restrictive, it also harmonizes. It is an order that allows humans to encounter one another at a human level. The order is not one *within* which humans live with submission; it is one *by* which humans express and confirm their own subjectivity creatively. By practicing according to the ritual propriety, people can transform what is regulative into constitutive.

Li as Effective Ways of Action

Being a practical man, Confucius was conscious of the utilitarian functions of ritual propriety. According to him, ritual propriety is a way in which human actions can be done properly and most effectively.

Not being mediated by the observance of the ritual propriety, in being respectful a person will wear himself out, in being cautious he will be timid, in being bold he will be unruly, and in being forthright he will be rude. (8/2)

The power of ritual propriety is so unusual and amazing that it can be considered "magical" (Fingarette, 1-17).[2] It accomplishes what one intends to do directly and effortlessly, without the use of coercion or any physical force. For instance, in public affairs, if those who are in superior positions are fond of ritual propriety, the common people will be easy to command (14/41), so easy that they will even follow without any command (13/6).

If there was a ruler who achieved order without taking any action (*wu wei* 無爲), it was surely Shun. What did he do? He simply assumed an air of respectfulness and faced due south.

That was all. (15/5)[3]

This is the Confucian notion of "action by non-action (*wu wei*),"—a notion more well known for its Daoist affiliation. While the Daoist notion of *wu wei* is to do things naturally and spontaneously, the Confucian notion is to accomplish intended results by ritual proprieties enlivened by moral virtue. It is non-action because the forces at work are invisible and intangible, and the person who does the action does not seem to be exerting any force at all. When a person walks toward another and reaches out her hands with a smile, the other will spontaneously turn toward her, return the smile, and raise his hands to shake hers. No coercion or command or any tricks, a cooperative action of greeting is done by the life of the ritual (Fingarette, 9), which embodies the respect and trust from the agents involved. In getting someone's attention, a loud "hey, you!" is more forthright and effective than a soft "excuse me" as far as the immediate purpose is concerned. But the lingering results of the two will be the opposite, and the subtle messages contained in the eventual effectiveness of the two go far beyond merely calling attention.

There is a class of linguistic actions called "performative utterances," the discovery of which is associated mainly with the works of J. L. Austin in the early nineteen-sixties. The utterances are not acts of descriptions about certain facts or acts of instructions to induce some other action; they are the very execution of the acts itself. A promise is a typical example. The utterance is the very act of promising. Other examples include excuses, commitments, compliments, pleas, and words that express our wish or preferences. By saying "I choose this one" in the proper circumstances the words constitute the very act of choosing. Fingarette says, "the lesson of these new philosophical insights is not so much a lesson about language as it is about ceremony," for all these acts are ceremonies or rituals or they are nothing. They cannot be done out of the context of certain settings.

> No purely physical motion is a promise; no word alone, independent of ceremonial context, circumstances and roles can be a promise.

> In short, the peculiarly moral yet binding power of ceremonial gesture and word cannot be abstracted from or used in isolation from ceremony. It is not a distinctive power we happen to use in ceremony; it is the power *of* ceremony. (Fingarette, 12 &14)

This observation further leads to the understanding that Confucius' doctrine of "*zheng ming* 正名," the "rectification of terms," is also of great importance for the practice of ritual propriety, for words are no less constitutive of effective ritual performance than gestures are.

For those who are interested in strategy, a story in the Analects can be very inspiring about how rituals can be utilized strategically. Yang Huo, a usurper in Lu, wanted to employ Confucius and Confucius refused to meet him. To meet him without being forced to would be a ritualistic act of recognizing the legitimacy of his reigning. Yang Huo then used a strategy by sending Confucius a pig. According to the ritual propriety of the time, the act obligated Confucius to return a courtesy call to the former to acknowledge the gift. Confucius waited for a time that Yang Huo would not be at home to pay the visit, but to his dismay, he encountered him on the road (17/1)! Though this kind of meeting does not count as a ritualistic recognition of Yang Huo's sovereignty, Yang's purpose was at least partially achieved by taking a small advantage of ritual propriety.

In light of what has been said, we find the appropriateness of the metaphor of *li*. For holy sacrificial rituals were used as a means to communicate with spirits, to obtain supernatural or natural consequences. Whether that kind of communication actually works or not, Confucius kept his mind open, but he saw that it really worked between humans.

Again, what was more important for Confucius was that ritual propriety not only works, it works in a way that promotes harmony.

> Achieving harmony is the most valuable function of observing ritual propriety. In the ways of former Kings, this achievement of harmony is the most wonderful. (1/12)

The harmony is not only in the public social-political realm; it is in the personal realm as well. According to Xun Zi,

> In matters pertaining to temperament, will, and understanding, one always gets through smoothly if one follows ritual propriety, and gets perverse, frustration, idle, or detainment if one does not. In matters pertaining to eating and drinking, dressing, dwelling, moving or resting, one always gets harmony and is in control if one follows the ritual propriety,

sacredness.

At a more fundamental level, the persons who are refined by rituals and the social order resulted from and exemplified by ritual proprieties can themselves be considered artistic. Refined by ritual propriety, a person will have the grace that enhances the natural beauty of the body profoundly. To the contrary, lacking proper manner, the natural beauty of a person will diminish dramatically, and in extreme cases, to nothing but what is of the flesh. An unsightly behavior is always opposed to ritual propriety, and a conduct in accord with ritual propriety is always elegant and aesthetically pleasing.

The beauty of the social order resulting from ritual propriety is compatible to the beauty of the natural world, in which objects are different but co-exist, rise and fall rhythmically. The beauty of each object is dependent upon its place in the whole, in relation to its environment, and not in isolation. The surrounding can enhance or reduce its beauty, depending upon how it is placed within the environment and between everything else. By ritual propriety, humans can correspond and interact with each other artistically, like performers in a well-trained orchestra, in which the artistic performance of each is aesthetically dependent on and enhanced by her cooperation with and coordination within the whole.

---

[1] I follow Ames and Rosemont's translation of the word "*li*" as "ritual propriety," for it captures the original metaphorical implications and the Confucian ramification of the original concept, mainly the process of making the tradition behind existing behavior patterns one's own, and the supposed quality of its being proper (see Ames and Rosemont, 51-2). When the word is used in a context that does not entail its "being proper," I shall just use "ritual" instead.

[2] The following elaboration of the point, and indeed the whole chapter, is deeply indebted to Fingarette's small book, *Confucius—The Secular as Sacred*. Those who are familiar with Fingarette's views will notice that, while I appreciate his insights greatly, I disagree with Fingarette's marginalization of the importance of *ren* and self-cultivation. My counter-arguments are implicitly entailed in my articulation of the Confucian theory, mixed with the points that I borrowed from Fingarette that I can agree with.

[3] Shun was an ancient sage king that Confucius revered greatly. South is the direction to which the superior's seats face.

5

Zheng—Social and Political Philosophy

This is the Confucian ideal society:

> When the great Way prevails, a public and common spirit is
> everywhere under the sky. People of talents and virtue are
> chosen, trustworthiness advocated and harmony cultivated.
> People love not merely their own parents, nor treat as children
> only their own children. The aged are provided till their death,
> the able-bodied all have places to utilize their ability, and the
> young have the means for growing up. Widows, widowers,
> orphans, childless, disabled, and ill, all sufficiently
> maintained. Men get their share and women have their homes.
> People hate to throw goods of value away upon the ground,
> but see no reason to keep them for their own gratification.
> People dislike not putting their strengths into use, but see no
> reason to use them only to their own advantage. Therefore
> schemings diminish and find no development; robberies,
> thefts, rebellions, and treason do not happen. Hence the outer
> doors need not be shut. This is called the Grand Union. (*The
> Book of Rites*, "*Li Yun* 禮運")

What is needed for achieving such a Grand Union is basically already laid out in the previous two chapters—*ren* (human heartedness) and *li* (ritual propriety). *Ren* is its substance and *li* its refined form. This chapter will serve more as elaboration and clarification of the principles as they are applied in the social-political realm.

Harmony vs. Conformity

The most impressive feature of the ideal society outlined above is its harmony. Confucius contrasted harmony (*he* 和) with conformity (*tong* 同). He says, "The exemplary person pursues harmony rather than conformity; the petty minded is the opposite" (13/23). Harmony is a state of co-existence and interaction between distinct participants. The different parts of a harmonious whole mutually blend in with each other and enhance each other without sacrificing their uniqueness. The parts forced into conformity are in agreement with each other where some of them lose their own personality and identity at the cost of enhancing others. People in harmonious relations *participate* in social activities and construction, not merely being *constituents of* them. They are motivated by their human-heartedness and they thrive through creative participation in artistic ritual propriety, without being made parts of a giant machine by legal or administrative enforcement.

A book composed before Confucius, *Zuo Zhuan* 左傳, has such a passage:

> Harmony is like broth. One uses water, fire, vinegar, sauce, salt, and plum to cook his fish and meat, …. If you add water to flavor water, who can eat it? If you keep playing the same note on the lute or zither, who can listen to it? The failing of conformity lies in this. (*Zuo Zhuan*, "Duke of Zhao, the 20th Year")

In political matters, if no one says anything different from what their ruler says, it is fine (though not good enough yet) when what the ruler says is good, but it would ruin a state if what the ruler says is not good (13/15). Duke Ai of Lu asked Confucius, "Isn't the son who obeys whatever his father says a filial son? Isn't a subject who follows whatever order his King issues a loyal subject?" He asked three times and Confucius remained silent. Afterwards, Confucius explained to his disciple Zi Gong: When a state has subjects who dare to stand up and appeal to the King, it will not be in danger. When a father has a son who dares to speak up, he will not deviate from ritual propriety. When a person has friends who dare to speak up, he will not take inappropriate action.

> Hence how can we say that the son is filial, if he obeys whatever his father says? How can a subject be considered loyal if he follows whatever his King orders? Those who examine what they are expected to follow, that is what filiation and loyalty means. (See Xun Zi, 29)

As it was impolite to go directly against the Duke, Confucius gave him a silent objection in the hope that the Duke would be able to figure it out himself.

"Exemplary persons are conscious of their own merits, but not contentious; they gather together with others, but do not form cliques" (15/22). They do search for real agreement on principal matters such as human-heartedness, the Way. "People who have chosen different ways (*dao*) cannot make plans together," says the Master (15/40). In terms of specific rituals, however, they will be flexible and appreciate diversity. Confucius would not, for instance, insist that a bow is more proper a ritual propriety for greeting than a handshake. His insistence on getting agreement on principal matters was also the search for unity, not partisanship.

Internal Sageliness and External Kingliness

Song Dynasty Confucian Zhu Xi 朱熹 comments on Confucius' distinction between harmony and conformity by saying, "Those who search for harmony have no ill-will; those who submit to conformity have the intention to please others." Ultimately, it is the self-cultivation that determines how one gets along with others. The harmony begins with one's own cultivation, and through that, the person will be able to regulate the family, govern a country well, and finally bring peace to the entire world. *The Great Learning*, one of the "Four Books" of Confucianism, has a famous formula:

> Those who wish to let their exemplary virtue manifest all under the sky must first order their own states well. Wishing to order their states well, they must first regulate their families. Wishing to regulate their own families, they must

first cultivate themselves. Wishing to cultivate themselves, they must first rectify their heart-minds. Wishing to rectify their heart-minds, they must first make their will sincere. Wishing to make their will sincere, they must extend their knowledge. Wishing to extend knowledge, they must first investigate things.

Within a family, if the parents set moral examples and put themselves in respectful positions, the rest of the family will follow. The magic power of human-heartedness and ritual propriety will transform the children intangibly. There is no need to have enforcement or coercion, and such is the environment within which the children can *grow*, not under which children will submit and survive.

Families are small societies on bases of which the larger society is structured. If one can be a good member of a family, she can be a good member of a larger community; if one can regulate the family well, she can rule a country well. When someone asked Confucius, "Why do you not actively search for a career in governing?" the Master replied,

the Book of Documents says, "It is all in filial conduct (*xiao* 孝)! Just being filial to your parents and befriending your brothers is carrying out the work of government." In so doing a person is also taking part in government. How can there be any question of my having actively taking part in governing? (2/21)

Extending the family model to the art of ruling, Confucius believed that the way to conduct *zheng* 政 (to govern) was to be *zheng* 正, a homophone that, when used as an adjective, means "being proper," "straight," "orderly;" and when used as a verb, means "to correct," "to make straight," "to put something in proper position." When a frame on the wall is tilted, it is "not-*zheng* 正" and should be "*zheng*-ed." The two words are not merely homophonous; they have an intrinsic affinity.

Being proper (*zheng* 正) in their own position, what difficulty would the rulers have in governing? But if not able to set themselves proper, how can they set others proper? (13/13)

Not only is *zheng* a necessary condition for ruling, it is also a sufficient one.

Ji Kang Zi asked Confucius about governing. Confucius replied, "Governing (政) is essentially just being proper (正). If you, sir, lead by being proper, who would dare be otherwise?" (12/17)

Since Ji Kang Zi was a ruler of the state of Lu, the conversation assumes the ritual setting—When someone in a ruling position is proper in his own conduct, the ruled would be proper as well. But the efficacy of a moral example is surely not restricted to those in a governmental position only. "The virtue of an exemplary person is like wind, and that of the petty person is the grass. As the wind blows, the grass is sure to bend" (12/19). In that sense, internal sageliness will not only qualify a person already in the noble position to be an effective ruler, it will elevate one to such a position by the power of influence. That is why Confucius extended the meaning of the term "*jun zi* 君子," which originally meant man of higher social status, to mean persons with morally exemplary quality. In some contexts the term is used deliberately in its double meaning. For instance, when Zi Lu asked about *jun zi*, he could have meant "What is an exemplary person like?" or "What should a person of high social status be like?" The answer is the same: "They should be those who become reverent by cultivating themselves." "By cultivating themselves, they will be able to bring peace and security to the people" (14/42).

Freedom

Confucianism has been blamed for being fundamentally authoritarian, paternalistic, and for imposing ritual propriety (*li*) to limit human freedom. In the works of Confucius and Mencius, there are no words close to the Western ideas of "choice" and "freedom." Meanwhile, there are apparently abundant codes in Confucian classics that put limits on what one can and cannot do, and even on what one can and cannot think or will. An individual is required to observe the traditional ritual propriety, to be filial to the parents, and to behave according to one's social status.

However, Confucius *does* uphold values that are expressed in the west by the term "freedom," though his views about the necessary conditions for freedom and how to achieve freedom are different from many other views on the same subject.

In his famous short autobiography, Confucius says,

At the age of seventy, I was able to follow my heart-mind's (*xin* 心) will (*yu* 欲) without overstepping the line. (2/4)

The message entailed in this short statement is quite rich, profound, and directly relevant to the topic of freedom. First of all, to "follow the heart-mind's will" is a state of "being free *to*" do what one wants, and of "being free *from*" constraints, restrictions, and coercion. If the "freedom *to*" is more about the freedom of the will, of choice, of the autonomy of the agent, the "freedom *from*" is more about the absence of restrictions. The "lines" of proper conduct still existed for Confucius at this stage, but they were no longer restrictive to him, for he had no tendency to overstep them any more. When one has no intention to rob a bank, the video monitors installed in the banks are no restrictions to the person; when one has no addiction to smoking, smoking regulations do not make the person uncomfortable. When a person has cultivated herself so well that there is no more desire to do anything immoral, she is free from moral restrictions in the same sense.

Second, the statement tells us that for Confucius freedom is achieved after or gained through cultivation, not a natural state that people are born into and can simply enjoy without having to earn it. In Confucius' own case, he set his mind at learning since the age of fifteen, and he was not free until the age of seventy. Though Confucius never denied the possibility of being born free entirely, he clearly would not say that it was common, just like he would not deny that one might be born with knowledge, but he said, "I am not one of this kind" (see 16/9 and 7/20). The process of self-cultivation involves the whole Confucian program of learning and practicing the Six Arts.

Third, the passage shows that for Confucius, the highest stage of freedom is not a state of indifference. It is a state of cultivated spontaneity. The dispositions gained from the cultivation, which include developed benevolent tendencies, ritual habits guided by rich knowledge and wisdom of how to apply them, etc., all become the person' s second nature, and enable her to act spontaneously and effortlessly in accordance with them. It is similar to the Daoist idea of *wu wei*— non-action, as illustrated by Zhuang Zi' s story of Cook Ding, who was, due to his long time practice, able to cut up an ox so skillfully that he can let his spirit move his arms and legs freely, like watching an event taking place by itself. In a state of indifference, however, a person is autonomous in the sense that he or she is not impelled by any inclinations or dispositions. It is true that if we limit the term "freedom" to the sense of being indifferent to inclinations, then Confucianism, and even the whole Chinese philosophical tradition, lacks this dimension. But there are compelling reasons to take the state of cultivated spontaneity as a more genuine state of being free than the state of indifference. One reason is that it does not seem possible for anyone to be free from dispositions. Secondly, even if we could, one who is totally indifferent would be like Buridan's ass, which starved to death between two equally good piles of hay because it could not find reason to go to one pile and not the other. After all, no matter how much one rationally deliberates, eventually one just has to let it go, and simply decide what to do. If one were to make a decision on the decision of a decision of a decision ... endlessly, one would simply be unable to make any decision, and this kind of state should be considered duly as, like Descartes puts it, the "lowest grade" of freedom. Descartes says:

> [T]his indifference which I feel, when I am not swayed to one side rather than to the other by lack of reason, is the lowest grade of liberty, and rather evinces a lack or negation in knowledge than a perfection of will: for if I always recognized clearly what was true and good, I should never have trouble in deliberating as to what judgment or choice I should make, and then I should be entirely free without ever being indifferent. (Meditations IV)

Once when he was commenting on whether one must think three times before taking an action, Confucius said: twice is enough (5/20). Clearly Confucius was aware of the fact that too much deliberation is restrictive, and having to deliberate too much is a sign of lacking freedom as well. Real freedom is found in getting out of indifference, in freeing oneself from difficult choices without blindly committing to wrong actions. That is possible only as a result of long time cultivation, which involves accumulation of experiences, learning rituals and customs, forming habits and dispositions, and not just as a result of deliberation. A good example is playing chess. A master looks at the situation, observes the opponent's move, and gives a certain amount of thinking. All these are done on the basis of the rich experience, knowledge, talent, and the ability of maintaining an optimal psychological and physiological condition. As a result, a good decision spontaneously comes. The master obviously enjoys more freedom than an uncultivated newcomer who knows nothing but "free self-determination" and holds a chess piece without even knowing how to deliberate.

The cultivated spontaneity entails more than merely the knowledge of relevant facts. In Western philosophy, Pythagoras, Plato, Spinoza, and Hegel, for instance, held the view that knowing the truth shall make a person free. Some scholars also tried to interpret Confucius' view of freedom in this way (see Graham 302), but ended up rendering Confucianism too intellectualistic. For Confucianism, it takes an all-rounded cultivation, most importantly, *ren* or human-heartedness, to be free. "Those who know are not perplexed," Confucius says; but that is not all. He also says that one must be *ren* to be free from worrisome, and courageous to be free from fear (9/29).

Fourth, the Confucian cultivation, as a way of achieving freedom, is primarily cultivation of oneself rather than fighting against others or removing external constraints. It begins with determination on learning. "If one sets strict standards for oneself and makes allowances for others when making demands on them, one will stay clear of ill will" (15/15; see also 1/16, 4/17, 15/21 and 20/1). Confucius even describes *ren*, the central quality of an exemplary person, in part as "reforming the self" (12:1). Confucian self-cultivation enables a person to be morally sensitive, compassionate, courageous, and wise. With these qualities, one is able to retain the mind undisturbed (*bu dong xin* 不動心) when one is confronted with seductions or threats.

To liberate oneself by working inwardly on oneself rather than outwardly toward conquering the external is actually common to all major Eastern philosophical traditions, despite their enormous differences from one another in their understanding of the self and on how to work on the self. Hinduism teaches that *Atman* (the true self) is identical with Brahman (the "self" of the universe), and to achieve freedom is therefore to live accordingly, namely, to eliminate the illusion that there is a self separated from and in opposition to the world. Buddhism denies the existence of a substantial self. To achieve freedom (mainly from suffering) is for the Buddhist essentially to live a selfless life. Daoism advocates the virtue of non-striving, of searching for harmony with the great nature. The way of pursuing the Dao is "daily drop"—drop one's desires or expectations, drop language, drop conventional knowledge, and drop even moral codes.

Confucius does not stress the importance of having alternatives to choose from and of the availability of information about options. His self-cultivation looks like a way of internalizing rules or indoctrination that restricts freedom. But the reason that Confucius would not stress these is not difficult to see: What one really needs is usually not the availability of many alternatives to choose from. Certainly one can choose to walk with eyes closed and hit the nose on a wall, but what is the meaning of the availability of this option? One can choose not to follow the traffic law and drive opposite to the traffic and run red lights and stop signs, but would that help one to get freedom to drive or to get killed instead, and never be able to drive at all? If what one really needs is not available, what do the other options matter to her? And before one can know and understand what is really good for herself, what good can the availability of some bad options do for her except to experience some painful lessons? Before one can reach the stage of cultivated spontaneity, one still needs to be constrained by "the line," and the line is a necessary guide for one to reach the stage.

Often Confucius' saying that "the common people can be made to follow a path, but not to know" (8/9) is cited, along with others, as evidence that Confucianism is authoritarian, and is opposed to human freedom and rights. But by this saying Confucius could not have meant that it would be better to keep the common people ignorant and powerless unconditionally. That would be inconsistent with his philosophy of education. Confucius would never refuse to teach anyone who sincerely wants to learn (7/7, 15/39). What he meant was that before a person reaches a certain level of cultivation, the person is unable to fully understand the reason for following the line. Therefore, pedagogically, the rulers (as the common people's guides) should first work on letting people follow the correct path rather than letting them understand it and have the power to go astray. His intention was very much like the intention behind today's movie ratings and drug regulations—until a person reaches a certain degree of maturity, it is for his own good to keep him away from seeing or having something, because the availability of these things tend to deprive the availability of the path that is genuinely good for him; in this sense, too much freedom is deprivation of true freedom. A person blind of what is really good for her, and is simply driven by desires and impulses, becomes a slave to these drives. Just look at how many people today end up being slaves to money and to their high-paying jobs—the availability of alternatives, especially that of a true liberal education—the path of becoming an authentic person, is dismissed by them on their way to reaching their dreams.

On the other hand, for those who have cultivated themselves well, and are able to interact with each other harmoniously, the emphasis of their freedom and right to choose is not only redundant; it may impair the very harmony itself. It would be silly and hurtful for a grown child

74

to claim to his mother that how he lives was his choice, and she had no right to give him advice. The idea of right entails a contractual relation to bind people externally, not a reciprocal correlative relation that connects people internally in harmony.

Fifth, the Confucian cultivation of the self aims not only at freeing one from negative and undesirable things or states, but also at obtaining an optimal state, gaining strength and power, and transcending one to higher levels of existence and experience. A well-cultivated person not only moves around freely, but also gets infinite resources around. As Mencius says,

> An exemplary person steeps himself in the Way because he wishes to find it in himself. When he finds it in himself, he will be at ease in it; when he is at ease in it, he can draw deeply upon it; when he can draw deeply upon it, he finds sources of help wherever he turns. (4B/14)

Sixth, the above point leads us to the realization that for Confucius, relatedness is essential in the Confucian account of freedom. This feature marks another major difference between the Confucian account of freedom and some most influential Western theories, such as Immanual Kant's and J. P. Sartre's. According to Confucius, not only is an individual unable to be isolated from others, whether the "other" is one's family, friends, neighbors, colleagues, rulers, the society, or *tian*—Heaven; one's relatedness to others is in fact a necessary condition for her to be free. Just like water is a necessary condition for one to swim, and adjusting one's body movement according to the nature of water increases one's freedom in the water, one's relationship with a specific environment is a necessary condition for the individual to be free within the given environment, and adjusting the relationship accordingly increases one's freedom in it. Separated from one's social relations, one cannot even talk about being free in the society. A free individual is not one condemned by "forlornness" which is accompanied by feelings of anguish and despair. The person is so inseparable from others that her domain of choice is itself defined and transformed by her interaction with others. Our specific others are not mere observers of our lives. When a person is facing a difficult choice between fulfilling two mutually exclusive duties, for instance, someone else's help may get the person out of the difficulty in the first place, leaving the person with no more conflicting duties to choose from.

Democracy

Partly because Confucianism lacked the right-oriented idea of freedom, the Chinese lived under the dominance of the state-sanctioned Confucian ideology, and suffered greatly from totalitarianism. Since Confucius grounded morality internally in the human heart-mind and in traditional ritual propriety, no religious submission to external deities was taken to be necessary, nor were the ideas of regulating human behaviors by external law and administrative measure taken seriously. Since the internal sense of *ren* and traditional ritual propriety are both up to each individual for interpretation, they are not as indisputable as commands from a god or a set of laws enforced by a government. Consequently, one has to rely on seeing whether one's own cultivated heart-mind is at ease or not as a test. When Confucius' disciple Zai Yu argued with Confucius over whether a three-year period of mourning was necessary, Confucius asked him whether he felt that his own heart-mind was at ease or not. When Zai Yu replied positively, the Master could do nothing but say "if that is the case, so be it" (17/21). While the self-disciplined and well-cultivated are able to take the stand by their own efforts, to transform themselves eventually to be part of the ternion, together with Heaven and Earth as a sacred being, the less cultivated still have to rely largely on external forces to stand up. Those who are reckless and selfish may even take advantage of this vagueness, which could be devastating if the individual is a ruler with no other restriction to his power.

The problem, reflected in the political realm, is the lack of a democratic dimension in Confucius' philosophy. The Confucian tradition was always concerned with how the ruler should offer benevolent government to the ruled, and lacked consideration of how the ruled might secure good government for themselves. It did not establish a structure for the ruled to actively participate in the governance. In Chinese history, Confucian political thought could do little more than reducing the harms of bad governments, and provided no effective measure for preventing them. Even morally conscientious emperors and ministers lacked an established social body or structure that was capable of supporting them and to ensure their success. Initiations of political change had to come from the imperial court rather than from the society. When intellectuals wanted to influence society, they had no means of doing so other than through influencing the imperial court.

While Confucianism does not entail the vision of a democratic social structure, is it compatible with democracy? Can Confucianism be interwoven with democracy?

Some argued yes. For Confucianism inherited the idea from *Shang Shu* (尚書, *the Book of History*) that the common people are the root or foundation of a society (*min wei ben* 民爲本). Statements such as "Heaven looks through the eyes of the people, Heaven listens through the ears of the people" in *Shang Shu* indicated that the common people were not taken as merely "the ruled;" they were the representatives of Heaven, above the rulers. This spirit is most distinctively reflected in Mencius' statement that "the common people are the most important; the spirits of the land and grain are the next; the ruler is the least important" (Mencius, 7B/14). Mencius also made it clear that the people have the right to rebel and to overthrow unqualified rulers.

Furthermore, it is believed that a democratic political system can be firmly established and fully utilized only when it takes a step forward to accept Confucian thought. The relationships maintained by legal rights are at their best external peaceful co-existences. They are not adequate for humans to develop and interact fully as humans. In the ideal Confucian society the ruler and the ruled are in morally reciprocal relation, not in a right-enforcement relation. When everyone is able to exert one's moral virtue to one's best ability, people will resonate with each other and forget the otherness on the basis of the common ground of being human. That is exactly the utmost ideal of politics. To interweave democracy into the Confucian moral tradition will change Confucian political thought from the standpoint of the rulers to the standpoint of the ruled, and establish a basis for political subjectivity of the common people. And to supplement democracy with the Confucian moral reciprocal relation and moral cultivation will make democracy a basis for a more superior ideal (Xu, 49-60).

Of those who believe that Confucianism and democracy are incompatible, there are different ways of looking at the incompatibility.

One view is that Confucianism is better than democracy. Democracy is based on the notion of human beings as rational, autonomous, rights-bearing individuals. This notion is contrary to the Confucian conception of human beings. Since it is an abstraction that leads us away from the actual concrete persons in social relations, it is fundamentally flawed. We do not choose in the abstract without "real hopes, fears, joys, sorrows, ideas and attitudes of flesh-and-blood human beings," nor do we choose as autonomous individuals who are solely responsible for becoming who we are ourselves. Our choices affect and are affected by the people to whom we have specific relationships. Furthermore, this notion entails no meaning of life, and therefore people have to look externally to find something that can make life meaningful. Confucianism, on the other hand, finds meaning of life right within our subjectivity. The ideas associated with the notion of right-bearing individuals, such as competitive individualism, are also far less humane than the human-heart driven and mutual nurturing of Confucianism (see Rosemont, 57-78).

A second view is that democracy is better than Confucianism. Some have argued that the traditional Chinese idea of "the people as the substance" does not extend beyond holding that the rulers should take common people's interest seriously. This idea still takes for granted that the government should be solely in the hands of the ruler, and that is the very opposite of the spirit of democracy and the government by law. It advises the rulers what they should do rather than saying what is required of them, and it is based on the premise that the people should *be treated* in a certain way, without placing them in a position to determine their own fate. The common people still have to rebel in order to overthrow repressive rulers. By expecting the ruler to treat the people as "the substance," the mentality of Confucianism is no different from that of the beggar who expects alms (Qi, 438-440).

A third view sounds somewhat in between. It recognizes that in an ideal Confucian society, there is no need and no room for rights. Between well-related family members, it is meaningless or even destructive to talk about their rights against each other. Confucians stress mutual responsibilities, not liberty; they stress self-control, not autonomy; and they stress paternalism, not equality. Yet it is an undeniable fact that the world, including China, is moving towards democracy. Instead of trying in vain to democratize Confucianism or to Confucianize democracy in order to produce a perfect ideology, we should try to see if the two may co-exist externally as value systems in the political realm (Li, 172-189).

One more alternative is to look at the issue from a historical perspective. A democratic system will not work for the good of its people until those who enjoy the rights have a minimum level of maturity to determine their own fate, and it will become unnecessary when the people who enjoy these rights can live together harmoniously. Yet between the stages, the stage that relies on sage rulers and the stage that harmony prevails, Confucianism must yield to or leave room for something less ideal—democracy. "We have to negate the tradition in order to reconfirm the ideal of the tradition" (see Liu, 1986).

At the time Confucius lived, common people were intensively tied to physical labor. They lacked the education, training, time and information necessary for them to participate in governmental affairs. It was therefore natural for the Confucians to expect the rulers to be paternalistic, and to provide the best guidance for the common people. While Confucius put more political power into the hands of the rulers, he also put more moral requirements and responsibilities upon the rulers. As we have mentioned before, the moral requirements are derived from the very notion of being a human, and are therefore more direct to a person than external constraints are. Furthermore, by editing historical records, Confucius established a moral supervision comparable to eternal blessing and condemnation. He imbedded moral judgements into the historical records so that the rulers would see that what they do, whether good or evil, will all be written down in history. To the Chinese whose notion of the self embodies the family and the community, the reward and punishment can be actually much graver than the affect on the person directly.

A country is like a family. When the children are small, we expect good parenting and good guidance for the children, even though it entails the exercise of authority and paternalism from time to time. When the children grow up, the parents should and are able to exercise more democracy, and respect the children's right to make their own decisions. Finally, the ideal state is that every member of the family is able to live in the family with a feeling of full participation, without the feeling of governing or being governed.

Women's Status

The least defensible part of Confucianism is its discrimination against women. Confucius says, "Only *nu zi* 女子and petty people are hard to rear. If you are close to them, they behave disrespectfully; if you keep a distance from them, they become resentful" (17/25). While the term "*nu zi*" can mean female children, or even be interpreted as maids, it has been interpreted mainly in later days to mean women in general. Furthermore, the term "petty people" is a moral classification, whereas *nu zi* is not. To classify the two together is also logically inappropriate.

However, there are several facts that may soften the blow and make our critical evaluation of Confucianism fairer. First, while it is undeniable and inexcusable that Confucianism on the whole oppressed women throughout its dominance in Chinese history, Confucius and his major successor Mencius, who did not enjoy the dominance, were not as degrading to women as their late followers. They never denied women's equal opportunity to learning and participation in state affairs. Confucius even agreed to meet the concubine of Duke Ling of Wei, regardless of her indecorous reputation, with appropriate ritual propriety to a person in a superior position (6/28). The distinction between men and women in early Confucianism was more a division of labor in the spirit of mutuality rather than in dominance. It was consistent with the general philosophical principle of harmony, rather than that of partiality.

Second, while the overall place of women in Confucian China was lower and subordinate to men, just like a subject was to a ruler, a younger brother was to an older brother, or a student was to a teacher, when it came to moral principles, self-cultivation, and personal contributions, a woman was not deemed by Confucianism necessarily inferior to a man. What Confucius said about teacher-student relations, "In facing with what is *ren*, do not yield even to your teacher" (15/36), could easily be applied to men-women relations. After all, a person's value and superiority is fundamentally derived from moral characters and contributions, not merely from sex. Anyone who visited Mencius' hometown at Zou County in Shan Dong Providence, China, would notice the prominent position that his mother held, while his father's position was hardly noticeable.

Third, as a mother or grandmother to her sons and grandsons, a teacher to her male student, or something comparable, a woman could be superordinate to a man in the traditional Confucian society. Empress Dowagers not only ruled the nation in the past, there are many still ruling households and beyond. The superiority or equality of these women was not derived from being women, but being a woman did not mean simply being inferior to men regardless.

Finally, Confucianism and feminism may even render support to each other. Both Confucian ethics of *ren* and the care-oriented feminist ethics focus on human relatedness and mutual care or nurturing; both emphasize situational and personal judgement, character building, rather than rigid rule-following; both recognize the importance of differentiation or gradation of one's duties toward others (see Li, 2000).

Given these considerations and the general principle of human-heartedness, it seems that the oppression against women needs not be taken as an indispensable part of Confucianism. To discard the discriminatory element and replace it with the idea of women's equal status is not only possible with Confucianism; it is arguably something we can do to make Confucianism more self-consistent.

6

Xue—Learning to be Human

Having laid out the basic outline of Confucius' philosophical system, let us now turn to the dynamic and holistic process of transformation of the person, the process of self-cultivation, and bring up some important points that yet need to be made clear.

Xue—Learning

Self-cultivation starts from *xue* 學. The word "*xue*" is usually translated as "learning." While the translation captures the basic meaning of *xue*, some precautions are necessary for getting an accurate understanding. First of all, "learning" usually entails an object to be learned, and it is an achievement verb. In the same way that "seeing" entails something's being seen (different from "looking"), "hearing" entails something's being heard (different from "listening"), "learning" entails something's being learned. *Xue*, however, is in this respect different from "learning." It is not an achievement verb. One may *xue* but not necessarily obtain anything. In some contexts it is more appropriate to translate it as "studying." Secondly, learning usually means to obtain something, whether "what" (truths) or "how" (skills). It is like adding something to the learner. *Xue* entails a stronger sense of affecting the person as a person, whether by improving one's sensitivity, understanding, or ability. The process of *xue* is the process of appropriating what is learned, the process of becoming and transforming.

As any self-transformation starts from the recognition of one's own ignorance and imperfection, Confucius repeatedly stressed the importance of learning. The Master said,

> Those who are born with knowledge are the highest. Next come those who attain knowledge through study (*xue*). Next again come those who turn to study after having been vexed by difficulties. Those among the common people, who make no effort to study even after having been vexed by difficulties, are the lowest. (16/9)

The Master did not mean that some people were actually born with knowledge. He just wanted to leave the possibility open. He said, "I am not the kind of person who is born with knowledge. Rather, loving antiquity, I am earnest in seeking it out" (7/20). "To say you know when you know, and to say you do not when you do not. That is knowledge" (2/17). Knowing one's own inadequacy is the condition necessary for becoming an authentic person.

In the pursuit of learning, one must first be motivated, and to be motivated, one must understand its importance. Speaking in general, to be fond of learning is to be fond of becoming an authentic human being, and the activity of the pursuit of learning is itself a distinctive feature of an authentic human. Biologically, human beings are similar in nature. It is by learning they diverge (17/2).

To speak more specifically,

> The flaw in being fond of human-heartedness (*ren*) without being fond of learning (*xue*) is that you will easily be fooled. The flaw in being fond of cleverness without being fond of learning is that you will likely deviate from the right path. The flaw in being fond of trustworthiness without being fond of learning is that you will be liable to lead into harmful behavior. The flaw in being fond of forthrightness without being fond of learning is that you will be rude. The flaw in being fond of boldness without being fond of learning is that it leads to unruliness. The flaw in being fond of firmness without being fond of learning is that it leads to presumptuousness. (17/8)

While Confucius never denied instruction to anyone who sincerely wanted to learn, he did not open the way to those who were not driven by eagerness, nor did he repeat himself for those who, having been pointed out to the East, did not try to figure out by themselves where the South, West, and North were (7/7, 7/8).

One must also be persistent in the course of learning. "There are indeed seedlings that do not flower, and there are flowers that do not fruit" (9/22).

As in piling up earth to erect a mountain, if, only one basketful short of completion, I stop, I have ended up incomplete. As in filling a ditch to level the ground, if, having dumped in only one basketful, I continue, I am progressing. (9/19)

Do I possess knowledge? No, I do not. If a rustic puts a question to me and my mind is a complete blank, I keep attacking the question from both ends until I have gotten everything out of it. (9/8)

One must furthermore not hesitate in correcting oneself when in error (1/8). "Petty persons are sure to gloss over where they have gone astray" (19/8). When he was told that he misjudged someone, the Master said, "I am fortunate. If I make a mistake, others are sure to inform me" (7/31). "When you erred and yet not to correct yourself, that is to err indeed" (15/30). Often the problem is that, when something goes wrong, people do not turn themselves to search for the answer. They tend to blame others or blame the fortune. Yet the exemplary person is like an archer who first searches for the fault within when he fails to hit the mark (*Zhong Yong*, 14; see also the *Analects*, 14/35).

As for the subjects of learning, Confucius' emphasis was clearly on how to be an authentic human, on what would contribute the most in person-making, though his aim was to constantly strive toward an all-inclusive perfection.

His education program, as we have indicated before, consisted of the Six Arts—ritual propriety, music, archery, charioteering, writing, and arithmetic. Ritual propriety is the training that enables the person to behave appropriately in accordance with what is right. It covers from the very basic manner such as the way one stands, sits, walks and eats, to complicated ceremonies. It enables a person to participate fully in human encounter and to build up healthy personal relationships, while at the same time transforming oneself. Those who have mastered ritual propriety will have physical grace as well as virtues inside of themselves.

The word for music is *yue* 樂, which actually covers dance and singing as well. Again, it is no less a means of building civilized persons and their harmonious relation with the surroundings, than a means of enjoyment. The Master's selection of music was strictly in accord with his vision of appropriateness and nourishment to the human person. His comment on one of the poems in the *Odes*, "The Cry of the Osprey," was that it was "pleasing without being excessive, mournful without being injurious" (3/20). His remarks about "Shao 韶" and "Wu 武," two works of music, were that the former was both superbly beautiful and superbly good, and the latter was superbly beautiful, but not equally good. The difference was that "Shao" praised the ancient sage kings, Yao and Shun, who ruled the kingdom by their moral virtues, and yet "Wu" praised King Wu's accomplishment in using military force to bring peace to the world (3/25). If we say that ritual propriety sets standards for human behavior and disciplines the body, good music promotes harmony within and between human beings (see *Book of Rites*, chpt. 19).

The arts of archery and charioteering are more physical than ritual propriety and music. Yet they are not without moral implications. An archer is supposed to ascend with proper greeting to others and descend, whether having hit the target or not, gracefully, and drink a salute to those who did. "Even in contesting, they are exemplary persons" (3/7). The *Book of Rites* tells us that in the ancient times, kings even selected their subjects for posts in archery competitions (chpt. 46). Similarly, Charioteering requires, in addition to the bodily skills of coordination and instantaneous reactions to the changing road conditions, the manner of driving as well. An educated person should not fight against others for a better road (see *Book of Rites*, chpt. 41).

The art of writing, *shu* 書, entails both calligraphy and composition. As in the way one stands, sits, and moves around, both calligraphy and article composition display a person's manner and personality. How one writes sometimes speaks as much about the person as what one writes about.

Of the Six Arts, arithmetic has least to do with morality, but through the training for quickness and precision, it also refines the person. The use of the abacus is an exercise both for the mind and for the body (the hands).

An obvious omission in the program is the natural sciences. Confucius felt close to nature, but he never displayed any interest in dispassionate, objective analysis of nature, like the scientists do. His remarks about nature are without exception objectification of his moral and aesthetic sentiments and virtues. As Xu Fuguan points out, the names of plants and animals in the three hundred *Odes* are sentiments and virtues of the poets, not botany or zoology. Western science interprets human as part of nature; Confucius interprets nature in terms of human—an interesting contrast that takes us back to what Xu said about the origin of the two cultures, one from a sense of curiosity and the other from a sense of anxiety.

Even though the Confucian spirit lacks a scientific dimension, Xu maintains that it does not mean that it is against science. It is rather that given the aim of the Confucian tradition, the methodology that it needs is different. What Confucius aimed at was the cultivation of the human and manifestation of the authenticity of human beings. That is why the selection of plum, orchid, bamboo and chrysanthemum as representatives of the four seasons reflects more moral ideals than features of the natural world (see Xu, 1952).

Two points in addition though, are that, first of all, it is questionable whether any science could be free from being value-laden and is not in some degree objectification of human values and assumptions. Modern science, for instance, is the objectification of the Bacon-Newtonian outlook that takes the natural world as an aggregate of discrete inert and mechanical entities with no intrinsic value. Based on this devaluation of the natural world, a model of human praxis is formed. Actions done out of this model tend to be hardly anything but manipulation, empowerment, and convenience.

Secondly, though Confucius never really delved into natural sciences, the holistic and correlative way of thinking that was prevalent in Chinese philosophy, including Confucius' teachings, have led to remarkable achievements and insights about how the universe (including our own body) functions. It is best exemplified in traditional Chinese medicine. Confucius' own observation about the connection between human-heartedness and longevity (6/23) and his followers' contribution to Chinese medicine and the Chinese theories of health are indications that Confucianism may have more profound understanding of how the natural world functions than modern medical science does, though the latter is indisputably much more advanced in detailed local areas. The most remarkable feature of the Confucian outlook of the natural world is that it helps us to understand the inseparableness between the body and the mind, between moral cultivation and the overall wellness of a person, and between the state of an individual and her interpersonal relationships (see Ni, 1996 & 1999).

Si—Thinking

Learning must be accompanied by *si* 思, thinking or reflection.

Learning without thinking, one will be perplexed; thinking without learning, one will be in peril. (2/15)

It is necessary for one to be reflective, to evaluate what one learns, and indeed, to select what to learn as well. Not everything out there or in the antiquity is equally worth learning, and what is worth studying may not be worth accepting. Facing all kinds of different theories and modes of praxis, if one were not being reflective, the more one learns the more perplexed one gets, as in the case of those who have "learned" and consequently gotten into radical relativism and nihilism.

On the other hand, the great minds of the past times and the world in general are resources that we cannot afford to ignore. Too much confidence and indulgence in one's own independent thinking without due respect for the knowledge and the wisdom passed on to us from others and to the rich life and the vast world around us is foolhardy and dangerous. "Once, lost in my thoughts, I went a whole day without eating and a whole night without sleeping," says the Master, "I got nothing out of it. I would have been better off devoting the time to learning" (15/31).

By *si*, Confucius means more than mere intellectual reasoning from premises to conclusions, or generalization from particulars to universal principles, or deliberation between alternatives. Those are surely basic operations of the mind, and Confucius' acceptance of them is evidenced by the saying that given one corner one should be able to come up with the other three (7/8), by the saying that his way can be summarized in one word, "*shu*" (15/24), and by the choice he made between following the majority or not in ritual formality (9/3). But for Confucius *si* involves the *heart* part of the heart-mind. The heart is engaged in the process of reaching a deeper understanding, of critical evaluation, and of appropriating what is learned so that one is able to apply it creatively and artistically.

This is the most distinctive feature of the Confucian way of thinking. As the heart is a part of the body that feels, in this sense, it is a bodily way of thinking!

Let us refer once again to the passage in which the Master commented on his disciple Zai Wo's attempt to reduce three years

86

mourning to one. The Master simply asked, "Would you feel at ease eating fine rice and wearing colorful brocade?" "Yes, I would," said the disciple. "If you would, then do it," said the Master.

> When exemplary persons are in mourning, they find no relish in fine-tasting food, no pleasure in the sound of music, and no comfort in their usual lodgings. That is why they do not [diminish the mourning period to one year]. Now if you feel comfortable with these things, then enjoy them. (17/21)

Here the way of thinking that the Master teaches is to introspect whether the heart-mind will be at ease (*an* 安). The subject brings whatever feelings and ideas that he encounters in front of the moral subjectivity in his own heart-mind, and examines whether or not he can accept the feelings or ideas at ease. In the same spirit, "*shu* 恕," the method of being *ren*, is also a thinking process that involves the body. In comparing one's own heart-mind with others' in a compassionate and empathic way, one observes whether it would be at ease to do something or not. When another disciple asked Confucius about exemplary person, the Master said, "The exemplary person is free from worry and apprehension. ···If there is nothing to be ashamed of upon self-reflection, what can the person be worried about and afraid of?" (12/4) It is worth quoting from Mencius again for further illumination:

> An exemplary person steeps himself in the Way because he wishes to find it in himself. When he finds it in himself, he will be at ease (*an* 安) in it; when he is at ease in it, he can draw deeply upon it; when he can draw deeply upon it, he finds sources of help wherever he turns. (4B/14)

It is no coincidence that the Chinese language contains lexicons that can be illustrative of the bodily characteristic of the Confucian way of thinking and knowing, as Xu Fuguan and Tu Wei-ming have pointed out. Experience is called "*ti yan* [體驗 bodily experience]," understanding is called "*ti hui* [體會 bodily understanding]," examination is "*ti cha* [體察 bodily examination]," knowing is "*ti zhi* [體知 bodily knowing]," and recognition is "*ti ren* [體認 bodily recognition]." The subject does not passively receive impressions, nor does she merely reason intellectually. She experiences with the body engaged, understands with her heart in empathy, examines with the sensitivity of the body. She knows with the active participation of the body, and embodies what is known.

Obviously Confucius would not say that one should just accept whatever the body likes or enjoys. It is the deep conscience (or "moral sense," "moral intuition," "moral subjectivity") in the heart-mind that one should bring up. So the process is both an affirmation of the self and a self-restraint 克己 (12/1). The result is the elimination of conflicting urges and inclinations, the heart-mind at ease, and the growth of moral subjectivity.

Zhi— Knowing

The entire process of learning and reflection involves the body, and thus requires practice to perfect. The outcome is not nearly as much an accumulated body of knowledge as a kind of ability. That is why some Song and Ming dynasty Confucians do not call Confucianism a doctrine; they call it instead a "*gong fu* 功夫." "*Gong fu*" in Chinese means both a way of doing something with genuine bodily effort, and a talent or ability that is usually obtained through receiving training from masters and through one's own diligent practice.

The fact has profound philosophical significance. It means that to conceive of Confucius as a philosopher in the common sense of the term is quite misleading. Confucius is not a philosopher who aims merely at creating a theory or an account of a philosophical problem. Philosophers of this kind may be good scholars, not necessarily exemplary persons, much less sages, which Confucius humbly says that he is not, though he is widely accepted as one of the most distinguished sages. A philosopher in the common sense is one who engages merely in the intellect, who possesses, again intellectually, some knowledge about the subject. In this sense, to be a Kantian, for instance, one only needs to accept what Kant believes, and thinks in a Kantian way. One is able to understand Kantian moral duty perfectly well without practicing it; for Kant's moral duty has nothing to do with dispositions. To be a Confucian and to understand moral duties in a Confucian way, however, requires more. For Confucius, true recognition of one's moral duty requires the person to bodily recognize it. In order to bodily recognize it one has to practice the method of *shu*. To practice the method of *shu* one must internalize it as one's second nature, so that not only one accepts it theoretically, but also forms inclinations towards it, dispositions to act in accord with it, and is skillful enough in ritual propriety to do it well. The person needs to practice the *gong fu* and embody the *gong fu* in order to even just understand it adequately.

Since the recognition of the duty is obtained through diligent practice and is fully embodied, the Confucian duty does not lack any necessity in its imperative power, nor is the Confucian subject less autonomous than a Kantian individual.

The fact shows that to interpret Confucianism merely from the intellectual perspective misses the very essence of Confucianism. Comparative philosophy is often done through finding similarities. While it is unquestionably worthwhile, it is easy to slip from finding similarities to assimilating what is distinctive. One may talk about Confucian metaphysics, for instance, and compare Confucius' notion of Heaven with Western philosophical concepts of the ultimate reality. But to reduce the Confucian notion of Heaven to a speculative metaphysical notion misses the nuance of it. Heaven, as we explained in the second chapter, is to be experienced directly, through introspection and decision, not speculation and postulation. Heaven is not an abstract metaphysical notion or principle; it is something immanently alive and concrete within every person. The recognition of Heaven is both an act of intellectual inquiry and an act of attuning oneself one with Heaven. There is no more separation of the knower and the known, of the act of knowing and the act of being and becoming, and even the act of "knowing what" and the act of "knowing how."

In light of the above explanation, we are able to see now the reason that Confucius taught his philosophy in his way—he never gave systematic lectures to articulate his views. Most of his teachings were given by short and direct instructions. Sometimes they were given by the Master's own way of living as an example. The *Analects* shows that when asked about *ren* by the disciples, Confucius never tried to describe *ren* per se. He talked about what a *ren* person would be like, how they would act, and he gave instructions according to each disciple's particular condition, letting them know on which level and which aspect they should start or continue their practice. The teaching method is indeed more typical of *gong fu* masters than of philosophy teachers in the common sense of the term. If he were to describe *ren* verbally, he would be misleading the disciples to a mere intellectual understanding, where the real spirit of *ren* would be absent, like seeing a shadow from the outside, or trying to scratch the feet across the booth.

The contrast between a *gong fu* master and a philosophy teacher is itself an interesting and important philosophical question that yet needs to be explored. The teacher-student relation from the Aristotelian tradition is based on the assumptions that human beings are essentially

89

rational beings, and true knowledge is rational knowledge, always describable and capable of being communicated by language. The primary function of a teacher is to train the students to use the reason already possessed by them. The way of instruction is to use words or other symbols to present facts, to persuade students by appealing to their reason through verbal clarification and argumentation. The student is encouraged to ask "why" and request a reason for everything he or she learns, unless it is seen by reason as self-evident. In the sense of possessing the faculty of reason, the student is not inferior to the teacher.

The *gong fu* master-disciple relation from the Confucian tradition, and indeed from other major Eastern philosophical traditions as well, starts from the assumption that true knowledge is much more than what words can convey, and requires much more than the intellect to perceive, to understand, and to appropriate. One's reason must be aided by cultivated intuition, by the awareness accessible only through direct experience. The master, being well-cultivated, is on a higher standing, capable of seeing things that are not accessible to the uncultivated disciple. What the master perceives cannot be conveyed to the disciple by words alone. So the disciples are taught in an entirely different way—not mainly by verbal presentation and persuasion, but by more individualized instructions that the disciples are supposed to follow—not merely to accept intellectually, but to practice accordingly. Sometimes the disciples are even discouraged to ask why, because without trying to experience what is to be understood, a verbal answer could easily mislead the student to think that he has already understood the answer from the words.

The evaluation of the two traditions is obviously dependent on the evaluation of the assumptions that each of them is based on. The Confucian would say what is perceived is certainly dependent on the state of the perceiver. Facing a cultivated master, the best position to take is to be an honest learner, and the worst is to presume that you already have all you need for knowing the truth, or even that you knew the truth already and you are capable of judging the masters. But Confucius differs from many "masters" in an important way. He did not ask his disciples to follow him blindly and to take whatever he said as absolute truth (see 7/31, 11/4). He instructed the disciples to draw deeply inside of themselves and from the tradition; he helped them to experience the moral subjectivity within and to elevate themselves to higher levels of perfection; and, finally, he encourages his disciples to be creative, for there are no rigid rules to follow.

90

Zhong Yong—The Mean

The Confucian *gong fu* culminates at *zhong yong*.

No excellence (*de* 德) is more supreme than *zhong yong* 中庸.
It has been rare among the common people for a long time.
(6/29)

"*Zhong* 中" means "centrality," "not to be one-sided." "*Yong* 庸"
has more complicated meanings. The major meaning of "*yong*" is
"ordinary," or "commonality." But it also means 用 (also pronounced as
yong)—"to function," "practicality," and *chang* 常, "constancy."
"*Zhong*" and "*yong*" are used together as one term, which is most
frequently translated as "the Mean." It is unrealistic to expect a
translation to capture the entire meaning of the original term; and even
the original term, short of careful articulation, has been taken
superficially to mean "never go to extremes," with an entirely
misleading and unfortunate connotation of "staying mediocre."

Centrality

There is considerable overlap between the Confucian doctrine of
zhong yong and the Aristotelian doctrine of the Golden Mean. Both
mean the virtue (not necessarily moral virtue), or excellence, of
avoiding two extreme vices—deficiency and excess.

> Zi Gong inquired, "Who is of superior character, Zi Zhang or
> Zi Xia?" The Master replied, "Zi Zhang oversteps the mark,
> and Zi Xia falls short of it." "Does this make Zi Zhang better?"
> asked Zi Gong. "Excess is as bad as deficiency," replied
> Confucius. (11/16)

> Hold truly to the middle way. (20/1)

But the middle way should not be understood as "staying between
extremes, regardless." To take the doctrine of the Mean, whether
Confucian or Aristotelian, in this way, misses the point entirely. The
advice is to stay between two vices, not between excellence and vices.
"Never stop before reaching the highest excellence" is in the very first

91

sentence of the *Great Learning*. The excellence of the Mean is itself the supreme excellence of hitting the right target, of staying where it is appropriate amongst the ever-changing situations and variations of conditions. The word "*zhong*" is therefore "appropriateness" in a more general sense than "*yi* 義" is. While *yi* is the appropriateness in moral matters, *zhong* applies to everything. To stay at *zhong* requires one to be in between the excess and the deficient, such as between being rash and timid, rigidity and spinelessness, conformity and antagonism, total attachment and complete indifference, callousness and fervidness. Those extremes are all vices that one should avoid. Neither extreme is better than the other. However, in regard to what is appropriate, *zhong* requires the utmost. It requires one to never be content with mediocre, the state of being merely "not too bad," and to never feel that one has done enough good.

Being a practical person, Confucius knew that it was unrealistic to require everyone to be perfect.

> If one cannot find the company of those who can travel at the mean (*zhong*), one has no choice but to turn to the rash or the timid. The rash will forge ahead in their actions and the timid will at least not do what they think is wrong. (13/21)

By retaining the merit of each and cultivating what is lacking, one can always move toward the Mean. Confucius' method of teaching was in tune with this aim. When asked about a same question by two different disciples, Zi Lu and Ran You, the Master gave opposite directions. With Zi Lu, he held him back, and yet with Ran You, he urged him to go ahead. Another disciple was puzzled, and asked the Master why. The Master replied, "Ran You is diffident, and so I urged him on. But Zi Lu has the energy of two, and so I sought to rein him in" (11/22).

The same art can be applied to all other areas as well. For instance in governmental affairs, if the existing policy is too lenient, proper amount of law enforcement should be introduced to balance the whole. In running a business, if the division of labor among the employees is too rigid, cooperation should be emphasized. In personal life, if the rhythm is too fast paced, one should then slow down a little. All one needs here is the simple extension of the logic—given one direction (say, the East), one should be able to figure out the other three (South, West, and North).

Commonality, Practicality, and Constancy

By associating "*zhong*" with "*yong*" Confucius brings the Mean more closely to the experiences and activities of the common people. Let us examine the three meanings of "*yong*" one by one and then bring them together.

"*Yong*" first of all means "commonality." The *Doctrine of the Mean* says,

> There is nothing more visible than what is hidden and nothing more manifest than what is subtle. (Chpt. 1)

The very secret of hitting the target of the Mean is hidden right in our ordinary experience—in letting the heart-mind be at ease, the *gong fu* that everyone has, yet few are able to perfect. The concept of "*yong*" makes the point clear that humanity underlies our common sense. In serving parents, in taking care of children, in respecting teachers, and in helping friends, the root of becoming an authentic person, or even a sage, is already there. The sage is just one who sees the significance of that which is common to us all, and is able to embody it and universalize it fully. The very commonality is the sacredness of human being, for the heart-mind at ease with appropriate conduct is Heavenly. By being one with it, one becomes co-creator of the universe. Yet the person still looks ordinary and amiable. He does not claim to have found something beyond the possibility of the common people.

However, exactly because humanity is hidden right in front of us in our ordinary common life, it is difficult to see. People tend to think that the profound should be obscure, the great should be beyond easy reach, and the sacred should transcend the secular. They would rather go to a monastery to pray to the invisible, rather than to seek within and around themselves for what they really need. The word "*yong*" is thus not merely a description; it is an instruction as well. It tells us where to look for the *gong fu*.

"*Yong*" also means "practicality." Though Heaven imparts the *gong fu* to every common human being, it is still a gift that needs to be earned or appropriated. One needs to cultivate oneself by practicing it diligently, let it function, and be in union with what is Heavenly in us. The practice should start right in our everyday common life. Those who do not see the importance of loving their family members and yet talk about universal love or the love of a supreme deity are like the ones who want to travel a great distance yet do not want to start from the nearest place (*Doctrine of the Mean*, chpt. 15).

Finally, "*yong*" also means "constancy." Everyone is able to live happily in union with his or her family members sometimes and behave altruistically in hostile situations occasionally. Yet it is rare to see anyone capable of being like this in his entire life. The real strength or *gong fu* of the well-cultivated is seen in her everyday activities that look trivial, unimportant. To have self-control is easier in alarming situations than in daily routine, in tiresome and trivial matters. In fact, self-control works only in situations where one realizes the need to have self-control. The real *gong fu* is to have no more need to have self-control. The appropriate action becomes so natural to the person that in doing so she feels that the action is a self-expression or exertion than self-control.

To bring the above three points together, we see that "*yong*" means the constant practice of what is common in human beings—humanity, that makes our heart-mind at ease when we do the appropriate thing. Since everyday life situations are dynamic and there is no rigid rule to follow, the person has to really embody the *gong fu* to respond to differing situations in a consistent way, and be creative, as a co-creator of the universe. After all, the unity between Heaven and human is not a combination of two entities. It is rather one's being true to her own Heavenly nature. "It is human that can make the Way great, not the Way that can make human great" (15/29), since the Way is made by human.[1]

Yue—Aesthetic Enjoyment

The fundamental aim of Confucian learning is to perfect oneself, and at the same time to perfect the world around. Ideally they should be one and the same, for the Confucian way of perfecting oneself is not solitary seclusion. But whether one can succeed in perfecting the world is not entirely up to the person. There is "*ming* 命," fate, which one has to recognize. The fate may sometimes be so unfavorable to the person that it repeatedly defeats her efforts in affecting the world. Confucius' own political career seemed to be exactly like this. He was known as "a person who keeps trying although he knows that it is in vain" (14/38). The reason that he kept trying regardless of the constant defeat, was that the Master had found the meaning or the worth of life right from within, from the effort itself, which was at the same time a source of aesthetic enjoyment.

The Duke of She asked Zi Lu about Confucius, but Zi Lu did not reply. The Master said, "Why didn't you just say to him: As a person, Confucius is driven by such eagerness to teach and learn that he forgets to eat, he enjoys himself so much that he forgets to worry, and does not even realize that old age is on its way." (7/19)

This kind of enjoyment makes fate, in a sense, irrelevant—having a good life is not dependent on having a good fate. "When the Way is in the view, let yourself emerge. When the Way is obscured, remain hidden" (8/13). Whether emerged or hidden, one just does one's best. As the famous Confucian saying goes, "When things go smooth, go and benefit the entire world; when not, the worst is that you can still perfect yourself as a result." The person enters an aesthetic realm, and life itself becomes artistic creation. The Master says,

I find inspiration from intoning to the songs; I learn where to stand from observing ritual propriety; and I find complete fulfillment in art and enjoyment (*yue* 樂). (8/8)

The word "*yue*" can mean either art or enjoyment, but in this passage it means both.

Set your sights on the Way, sustain yourself with virtue, learn upon human-heartedness, and wonder (*you* 游) in the arts (*yi* 藝). (7/6)

Unlike common conception of art that associates artworks with studios and galleries, the Confucian art is the artistic way of life itself. If a master of conventional arts is one who dissolves the opposition between the mind and the "hands," and between the hands and the objects that his hands work on, the Confucian aesthetic life is one in which the person has achieved the unity with Heaven, and is able to participate with Heaven in creation. The person has embodied *zhi*, knowledge or wisdom, and is therefore not perplexed; she has embodied *ren*, human-heartedness, and is therefore not worrisome; she is courageous, and is therefore not timid (9/29). The person enjoys water, for wisdom is like water, dynamic and creative. The person enjoys mountains, for human-heartedness is like the mountains, enduring and full of dignity (6/23).

Because this aesthetic spirit originates from deep within the person, it fills every corner of one's life, not just in dealing with some particular forms of art. The person may not be considered a prominent artist, for prominent artists are usually famous for certain things they do aside from their own personal life. The Confucian artistic creation, on the other hand, is displayed in the entire life, including ordinary daily activities. While the person may not be considered a prominent artist in the conventional use of the term, she is truly prominent (see 12/20).

And unlike Plato, who considers art as a preparatory stage in the progress toward true knowledge, knowledge of the immutable, permanent world of pure forms, Confucius takes the ever-changing, concrete artistic life itself as the living soul of the ultimate and the eternal. For this kind of life entails what makes life worth living. If "upon hearing the Way in the morning, the person can face death at dusk" (4/8), then a person who has lived in rhythm with the Way is surely able to say at the time of death that "I have not spent my life in vain."

The self-sufficiency of this aesthetic life should not be taken to mean that Confucius cares nothing about the utilitarian consequences. People usually take "non-utilitarian" as a distinctive feature of aesthetic activities. Yet a distinction must be made between the "non-utilitarian" feature of an *aesthetic* activity and the aesthetic *activity*'s being non-utilitarian. It is true that there is a non-utilitarian, aesthetic dimension in the Confucian way of life, yet it does not mean that the way of life has no utilitarian functions. In fact the unity between life and art entails the unity between utility and aesthetic appreciation. Confucius' "Knowing that it cannot be done and yet still keeps trying" is at its best when he "takes pleasure" in doing it.

Confucius' pursuit started from "the sense of anxiety" and completed with the contentment so fully that he "did not even realize that the old age is on its way" (7/19). The secret, to put it in a single expression, is that he found a way to unify the human with Heaven.

---

[1] Readers should refer to Tu Wei-ming's book, *Centrality and Commonality*, for more thorough articulation of the subject.

Bibliography

Ames, Roger T. and Rosemont, Jr. Henry, 1998: *The Analects of Confucius: A Philosophical Translation*. New York: Ballantine Books.

Book of Rites, (Li Chi) 1967: trans. by James Legge, New Hyde Park, NY: University Books.

Chen, Wing-tsit, 1963: *A Source Book in Chinese Philosophy*, Princeton, NJ: Princeton University Press.

Confucius, The *Analects of Confucius*. See Ames and Rosemont.

de Bary, Wm. Theodore, 1991: *The Trouble with Confucianism*, Cambridge, MA: Harvard University Press.

Doctrine of the Mean, 1971: in James Legge trans. *Confucian Analects, The Great Learning & the Doctrine of the Mean*. New York: Dover Publications.

Dong Zhong-shu, 1936: *Chun Qiu Fan Lu,* in *Si Bu Bei Yao*, Shanghai: Zhong Hua.

Fingarette, Herbert, 1972: *Confucius —The Secular as Sacred*, New York: Harper & Row.

Gewirth, Alan, 1980: "The Golden Rule Rationalized," in *Midwest Studies in Philosophy*, Vol. III. Minneapolis: University of Minnesota Press.

Graham, A. C. 1989: *Disputers of the Tao,* La Salle, Ill.: Open Court.

Hall, David L. and Ames, Roger T., 1987: *Thinking Through Confucius*, Albany, NY: State University of New York Press.

Kant, Immanuel 1981: *Grounding for the Metaphysics of Morals*, Translated by James W. Ellington. Indianapolis, IN: Hackett Publishing Company.

Kupperman, Joel J. 1999: *Learning from Asian Philosophy*. New York / Oxford: Oxford University Press.

Li, Chenyang 1999: *The Tao Encounters the West*, Albany, NY: State University of New York Press.

———— 2000: ed. *The Sage and the Second Sex— Confucianism, Ethics, and Gender*. Peru, IL: Open Court.

Mencius, 1970: *Mencius*, trans. by D. C. Lao, Penguin Books.

———— 1970: *The Works of Mencius*, trans. by James Legge, New York: Dover Publications.

Mou, Zongsan (Mou, Tsung-san) 1963: *Zhongguo Zhexue de Tezhi* [中國哲學的特質 *The Uniqueness of Chinese Philosophy*]. Hong Kong: Rensheng Publishing Company.

Ni, Peimin 1996: "A Qigong Interpretation of Confucianism," *The Journal of Chinese Philosophy*, 23(1), 79-97.

———— 1999: "Confucian Virtues and Personal Health," *Confucian Bioethics*, ed. Ruiping Fan, Dordrecht / Boston: Kluwer Academic Publishers.

Qi, Liang, 1995: *Xinruxue Pipan* [新儒學批判 *Critique of Neo-Confucianism*]. Shanghai: San Lian Shudian.

Reid, Thomas 1846: *Complete Works of Thomas Reid*, ed. Sir William Hamilton, Edinburgh: Maclachlan and Stewart.

Rosemont, Henry Jr., 1991: *A Chinese Mirror, Moral Reflections on Political Economy and Society*, La Salle, Ill.: Open Court.

Tu Wei-ming, 1989: *Centrality and Commonality*, Albany, NY: State University of New York Press.

Sun Xing Yan & Guo Yi, 1998: *Kong Zi Ji Yu Jiao Bu* [孔子集語校補 *Collected Sayings of Confucius, Proofread and with New Additions*]. Shangdong: Qi Lu Shu She.

Xu, Fu Guan, 1952: "Rujia Jingshen de Jiben Xingge jiqi Xianding yu Xinsheng" [儒家精神的基本性格及其限定與新生 Basic Characteristics, Limitations, and Revival of the Confucian Spirit]. *Minzhu Pinglun* [民主評論 *Democracy Forum*] vol. 3, supplement to no.10.

———— 1980: *Xueshu Yu Zhengzhi Zhijian* [學術與政治之間 *Between Politics and Scholarship*]. Taipei: Student Book Company.

Xun Zi, 1967: *Basic Writings of Mo Tzu, Hsun Tzu, and Han Fei Tzu*, trans. by Burton Watson, New York: Columbia University Press.